Throw a Great Party

Throw a Great Party

INSPIRED BY EVENINGS IN PARIS WITH JIM HAYNES

MARY BARTLETT, ANTONIA HOOGEWERF AND CATHERINE MONNET

ILLUSTRATIONS BY TRISH NICKELL

iUniverse, Inc.
New York   Lincoln   Shanghai

Throw a Great Party
Inspired by evenings in Paris with Jim Haynes

iUniverse books may be ordered through booksellers or by contacting:

iUniverse
2021 Pine Lake Road, Suite 100
Lincoln, NE 68512
www.iuniverse.com
1-800-Authors (1-800-288-4677)

Because of the dynamic nature of the Internet, any Web addresses
or links contained in this book may have changed
since publication and may no longer be valid.

Illustrations© Trish Nickell
www.trishnickell.com

Cover Design by Annabelle Adie,
www.annabelleadie.com

Photo credit: Mechthild Holter 1987 Photograph of Jim Haynes

ISBN: 978-0-595-43789-4 (pbk)
ISBN: 978-0-595-88119-2 (ebk)

Printed in the United States of America

Acknowledgments

In every aspect of creating this book, Paul Allman's contributions have been outstanding and deeply appreciated. The authors are grateful for his steadfast encouragement, vital editing and research, and his discriminating taste in food, wine, and entertaining.

A simple thank you seems a pale response in relation to our tremendous gratitude.

By virtue of their help and unique additions, we especially wish to acknowledge the input of Betsy Allman, Jessica Buck, Claudia Bushee, Ernesto Buttafoco, Miriam Camitta, Lolly Chomowicz, Susan Derecskey, Susan Lindeborg, Maureen McCarthy, Yves Monnet, Terry Rye, Barbara Sherman, David Szafranski, and Michelle Yurick. We could not have finished without your help.

To all other volunteers and friends who have aided in the completion of this multicultural feast of a project, we are and continue to be profoundly grateful.

This book is dedicated to Jim Haynes and the more than one hundred thousand guests who have attended his Sunday night dinners.

Perhaps it could go unsaid, but without the inspiration of Jim, we could not have written this book for you, dear reader.

Mary Bartlett
Antonia Hoogewerf
Catherine Monnet

Table of Contents

Foreword

I want to thank Antonia, Catherine, and Mary for coming up with the idea of a book inspired by what has been nearly a thirty-year-party. A series of serendipitous events got the whole thing started and it's been a great ride ever since. Over 100,000 people have dined at my atelier in Paris, been introduced to each other, have become friends, lovers, married, and produced children. Well, not all of them. But many. Jobs and apartments resulted. Trips made. And now this book.

Starting with their own recipes and collecting others from past meals, they have pooled their extensive knowledge about entertaining to write a terrific book that captures what the Sunday night dinners are all about. I know this book will encourage you to throw a great party. Have a good time!

Jim Haynes
Paris

Young Jimmy and a friend in 1987

Introduction
to
Jim Haynes of Paris and his Great Parties

I love humans, men and women alike, no matter their age, profession, or nationality. For me each person is a country, a fellow Earthling, and I hope to explore and to begin to know everyone out there on this crazy planet of ours.

Jim Haynes

I'd love to see you; what was your name?

Jim Haynes

A few years ago, I found myself chopping a large pile of onions in an old artist's studio in Paris. Along with some other peelers and choppers, I was preparing food for one of Paris' best-known underground parties: the Jim Haynes Sunday night dinner.

In 2001, my husband and I spent a sabbatical year in Paris. Within a few weeks of our arrival, a French friend told us about Jim's dinners. "There's this American who has been giving big Sunday dinners for the past thirty years. He's not far from you and you'll meet all kinds of interesting people. You should check it out!" Our curiosity was piqued so we called and got our names on the list for the following Sunday. We were amazed at the size of the crowd (up to one hundred guests), the size of the space (small), the remarkable people, and the good food. Soon I learned that the cooks were a fluid group of volunteers who turned out to be visitors, houseguests and sometimes, cooking students. I had recently given up a small catering business and had a nostalgic longing to cook for a crowd. I asked Jim if it was possible for me to help with the cooking and he welcomed me onboard. Given my experience, I felt pretty confident that I could actually pull it off.

What I discovered was that Jim's friends who take on the cooking, do a wonderful job without any particular expertise or entertaining experience. This showed me that throwing a large party does not require a caterer, a chef, a professional kitchen, or even a large space. In fact, my catering experience was not that big an advantage.

As a guest and a cook at Jim's dinners, I became convinced that anyone can have a huge party and have fun doing it with a minimum of space, fuss, and expense. Unlike Jim, no one would open their home to a crowd every Sunday, but all of us have occasions to give parties. Your wedding, class reunion, bar mitzvah, neighborhood picnic, or your great-aunt's wake, all constitute a genuine excuse for a shindig that you can do yourself.

Through Jim and in his kitchen, I met Antonia Hoogewerf and Catherine Monnet who cooked regularly at Jim's and had years of experience in home entertaining. We discovered a mutual interest in writing about home parties. We began the project by collecting the most popular recipes we'd made for a crowd and asking for more recipes from people who have cooked at Jim's. We got loads of responses; not simply recipes but ideas and suggestions for all aspects of giving a party. What came through loud and clear was that throwing a large party at home is not hard to do and that the whole experience is fun.

A meal à la Jim Haynes will never be confused with a catered event. It is definitely home-style and that, undoubtedly, is its charm. In writing this book, I, along with Antonia and Catherine, want to show how to have an informal party without the guesswork and anxiety that many feel about entertaining.

Throwing your own party is generous and bighearted and people appreciate it. Your guests are there to enjoy themselves and they will. They won't remember if the toast got burned but they will remember what a terrific time they had. So, an important aspect of throwing your own party is to keep in mind the fun your guests are having. This will help you relax and enjoy it yourself.

While my professional cooking and catering experience was not the key to giving a party, it has helped me describe the process. Because of my work in the world of restaurants and catering, I understand and can explain why recipes succeed, how food shopping and storage works, and what planning and organization do for a party. It's all common sense and nothing that you couldn't eventually figure out for yourself but if you're nervous or mystified about throwing a party, this book might help get you over the hurdle.

The recipes are an ethnic hodgepodge (not unlike the guests at Jim's parties). From American homespun to French classics by way of Greece, Italy, India, and Thailand, the recipes are for home kitchens, have been tested many times, and guests love them. You can choose to make the recipes in either smaller or larger quantities. The chapter on how to plan and organize will show you how to host your own party from start to finish.

No one can be more of an inspiration as a host than Jim Haynes. Described as the ultimate networker, sweet Southern Jim Haynes has done remarkable things in his life, including founding the Traverse Theater in Edinburgh, the Arts Lab in London (where John and Yoko had an exhibition), co-founding the UFO club (where Pink Floyd was the house band), writing a lot of books (*Hello I Love You!* and *Thanks for Coming* to name two), and a thirty year stint as a university professor in Paris. But he has become best known for having the longest running dinner party ever. Jim, *the* American in Paris, welcomes old friends, new acquaintances, and utter strangers to his atelier for a meal and a chance to meet a lot of people.

The story of how the dinners started is essentially a tale of how a good party just kept getting bigger. Back in 1978, Catherine Monnet, a young ballet dancer from Los Angeles, needed a place to stay and through a friend, found her way to Jim Haynes.

"I arrived at his atelier around lunchtime and I made an omelette for him. He immediately suggested I stay until I found work and a place of my own. Was it my cooking? I have no idea but to repay his hospitality and contribute something to the household, I offered to cook for his guests. The thing just took off!"

At first, the dinners were small but over time, they grew to include eighty or ninety guests who pay a contribution toward the food costs. They have become famous for the start of friendships, love affairs, and marriages. People have found places to stay, new jobs, and opportunities for travel by participating in a Sunday dinner. How do people learn about these dinners? Word of mouth (absolutely no advertising) and a large and growing number of newspaper and magazine articles. Recent articles from the Chicago Tribune, Seattle Times, Frommers.com, and various in-flight magazines have motivated throngs of visitors to attend Jim's dinners. A friend of Jim's, Christopher Olsen, had this to say:

"Sunday nights at Jim's 21st Century salon may not quite rival those of the great literary intelligentsia of 19th Century Paris but in this anxiety-filled, Internet age, he is still making a profound statement. You cannot e-mail a conversation without missing the most important ingredient: non-verbal interaction. How about that flirt, that tease, that frown, that smile? All part of a few hours of conversation with mostly strangers."

You may not be entertaining a roomful of strangers but Christopher Olsen's words say a lot about what a party signifies. Your party can have this kind of energy because people love to be entertained. There's a level of comfort and a willingness to unwind that simply does not exist in restaurants or bars. With no check to pay and no pressure to vacate a table, guests feel happy and pampered (especially after a good meal). When you give a party, people get together, whether as old friends or new acquaintances. They talk, laugh, and generally have a good time. Sometimes wonderful things happen from there.

So, enjoy this book and above all, throw a great party!

THINK I'LL HAVE A PARTY ... NOW WHAT?

PLANNING AND ORGANIZING YOUR PARTY

It is, needless to say, a wonderful dinner. We are 37 men and 45 women for a grand total of 82. And we feed four neighbors! A great mixture of people once again.

Jim Haynes

Let's get the party started!

Pink

Scenario #1

It's your third marriage. You and your spouse-to-be have loads of friends who want to celebrate but are sick of giving you salad spinners. You can't face another wedding cake.

Scenario #2

Fifty-five cousins are showing up for a family reunion. Five of them offer to help with a picnic supper.

Scenario #3

Your friend, Jim Haynes, happens to be visiting and wants to see a few friends. You hope your village will hold them.

So, you're thinking of having a party. Now what? Time to make a plan.

Choosing the Location … Your Home!

A fourth, and more likely scenario is a party for twenty or thirty friends whom you would like to entertain in your home and provide with a meal. Will they fit in your space? Even without the slightest idea of the size of your home, my answer is yes.

It is not surprising that many people can fit in a small space and have fun (been to a rock and roll bar lately?) In fact, a crowded room is incredibly important for a successful party. Here's why: if people are all sitting down, things can be very quiet. As more people arrive and chairs get scarce, most stand up, move around, and get close. Suddenly, the place livens up.

So don't underestimate how many people you can cram into your living room (or garage or back yard). All those famed love affairs that have started at Jim Haynes's dinners? Inevitable when you're four inches away from your dinner partner. Do not feel you must provide a chair for each guest. At informal parties, people will naturally form little groups, drape themselves on your couch, sit on the floor, or lean against the wall. You do need one bathroom (with some extra toilet paper). If your home has a lot of furniture, especially small tables or groupings of chairs, think about putting some of it out of the way for the party. A good friend recounted:

> "I've been to parties where I was caught in a cul-de-sac and couldn't move to get a drink or food and watched as people stumbled over low tables and fell into big upholstered chairs."

Who's coming?

For most of us, gathering a huge crowd is not a routine event. Put plainly, you need to ask people to your party. People frequently accept an invitation and then forget all about it. Worse, they never respond but come anyway. Call it brain dysfunction or bad manners; it hardly matters. The point is you need to know as closely as possible how many guests you can expect. Whether by e-mail, telephone or invitation, make a list and ask for RSVPs. Jim Haynes's dinners are nearly an institution: people call, the list fills up and often there's a waiting list. Even so, he talks to every person to confirm acceptance. It's a good practice: don't be afraid to follow up with a phone call or e-mail close to the day of the party to confirm your numbers.

Once you know how many are coming, focus on who these guests are. A lot of your menu, bar and serving decisions will be based on your crowd. With a very large crowd, you may want to pick a menu that can be made ahead and served at room temperature. A smaller crowd? You might want to have some tables and a self-serve buffet. You will see that the recipes in this book are for twenty-five or one hundred servings. What's crucial is to match 'servings' to 'people'. Twenty-five servings are fine for an adult crowd of twenty to twenty-five. Teenage boys? Twenty-five servings will feed less than ten if they've just come from soccer practice. (Always, *always,* have plenty of bread if you have young men in your crowd). A non-drinking crowd eats more than a drinking crowd. An elderly crowd eats less than a middle-aged crowd but there are exceptions. An all-female crowd? Very few will have seconds. If in doubt, err (a bit) on the generous side but don't go overboard. You want just enough for some leftovers. Dealing with tons of uneaten food will make all your effort seem wasteful rather than triumphant.

So figure out a realistic estimate of the drinkers and eaters that will be coming to your party and move on to money considerations.

Budget (or juggling desire with practicality)
What do you want to spend in total? Food is just a part of the total cost, so include liquor costs and any other expenses (such as rental equipment, decorations, flowers, etc.) in your calculation. Break out what you can spend for food and divide it by the number of guests. That figure per person will help you to narrow down the menu choices. Will you have a green salad or asparagus? Veal stew or pasta? Is

your target three dollars per person or twenty? This takes a little time and snooping around the stores to figure out but don't skip this part. You want to have a party not a crushing financial blow.

The date of your party is important for determining your menu. Buying food in season and planning a menu around it is a big budget consideration. Asparagus in December? Very costly. Tomatoes in August? They're giving them away. From the standpoint of guests, a menu that fits the season and the climate are well appreciated.

At this point, are you crying out, "I want Champagne, damn it!" Your desires are important. Juggling your desires with your budget is the key. If your budget is more of a beer budget, then buying Champagne will seriously eat into the food part. So, how about a less expensive sparkling wine like Prosecco? Sometimes a compromise is a beautiful solution: Prosecco is not Champagne but it is very good wine with which to toast and celebrate. If you are dead set on Champagne, then go for it, but remember to trim in other areas if you intend to stay within budget.

Organizing your time
Once you've determined where your party will be, who's coming, and what you can spend, turn your mind to what you need to do in advance. Preparing a meal for a large crowd takes a total of twelve

to fifteen hours. If your schedule permits, the shopping, cooking, and setting up can be spread over several days.

There is no one *right* way to organize your time. The main thing is not to leave it all for the last day. Just as the cooks at Jim's have different ways of working out timing, you will be able to judge what is best for you. The more complex the menu, the more time you will spend preparing the meal. For example, if the dessert is ice cream and store-bought cookies (which people love, by the way), you will be spending less time than if you baked cakes.

Antonia Hoogewerf who cooks often at Jim's has this approach to a big job:

"The thing that gets you at first is the sheer quantity of food required and the time it takes to prepare it. If a recipe says, "Slice an onion" that's one thing, but slicing twenty onions takes serious time. If the recipe says "Brown the chicken pieces" this would normally take a few minutes, but twenty-five pounds can take over an hour. I like to do most of the cooking a day ahead. Anyone around is roped in to help and working steadily, it takes most of the afternoon."

A very large party is difficult for one person to handle alone. For twenty-five guests, two people to share or divide the shopping, cooking, and setting up are ideal. For fifty to one hundred guests, count on four: one cook, one shopper, and two prep cooks. Sometimes, the working time can be divided between several cooks so that one person is responsible for the appetizer, one for the main dish, and another for dessert. If you are highly organized, baking, cooking, and freezing in advance are good options.

You and a couple of friends may be doing the cooking for your party but who is going to serve? It is hard to do both unless you do all the cooking in advance and have some time to relax the day of your party. Generally, you will need three people to serve a large crowd; two to serve and one 'roamer' to pick up plates and glasses and stock the bar. Two helpers will work for a crowd of twenty-five to thirty people. With a comfortable relaxed crowd of friends, you will get some spontaneous help but don't count on it. You will be more relaxed if you have confirmed that one or two people will perform these important tasks.

Delegate as much as possible when it comes to decorations. For a no-fuss, informal party, a reasonably clean house and a place to put the coats are all that matter.

Coming up with a menu

The next step to throwing your party is coming up with a menu. You need to think carefully about how your budget may affect your menu choices. Here are some considerations:

For example, you may have vegetarian guests. It is always considerate to have some non-meat dishes on your menu. Selecting a main course such as Green Lentils and Sausages (p.88) where the meat is cooked separately is one solution that your guests will appreciate. That said, do not worry about accommodating specialized diets. This is the responsibility of the individual who accepts your invitation and he or she will probably ask you to point out any dishes that pose a problem. That is all you need to do for your guests to be comfortable.

Be sure that what is on your menu is compatible with your space and the size of your crowd. Even hot soup is manageable for a stand-up crowd as long as the bowls are not so thin that they are too hot to hold. Food that requires a knife, however, will not work if your guests are going to be standing. Let's put it another way: stand-up parties are fork-only occasions.

Does your brother have a strawberry farm? Are you expecting a bumper crop of apples? Take advantage of any seasonal foods that are available to enhance your dinner. Recipes such as Baked and Unbaked Tomatoes (p.109), Homemade Applesauce (p.141), Fruit Crumble (p.144), Zucchini Soup (p.34) and Strawberries in Balsamic Vinegar (p.149) are good ones to choose if you have access to a lot of fruits and vegetables in season. These are considerations that will have an effect on your menu.

To get some ideas, look at the sample menus that follow this chapter and then read some of the recipes carefully. Look carefully at the instructions and notes. Many of the recipes will state that they are easy to make or can be made in advance or that no oven is required. Strawberry Refrigerator Cheesecake (p.134) and Southern Banana Trifle (p.148) are examples of make-ahead desserts that require no baking. Be realistic about your time and space if you choose baked items. In some recipes, such as the divine Chocolate Armagnac cake (p.128) or Pain d'Épice (Honey Spice Cake) (p.132), baking in advance enhances the flavor.

Choosing Wines

Large informal parties do not lend themselves to complicated or expensive wine choices. However, reasonably priced wines that compliment the food are easily available. You will notice that wine suggestions follow the recipes for the main dishes. Use these as a general guide but don't fret about *perfect* pairings. Beaujolais (Gamay) is an example of a light red wine that goes very nicely with many different kinds of main dishes and isn't a budget buster.

Boxed wine is an excellent choice for a large party. It is by far the easiest, self-serve choice at a bar. In France, boxed wine is often far superior to bottled wine of the same price. The same is starting to be true in the United States but you need to know your local wine merchants and their products.

A few words of explanation about the wine suggestions: you will be given a general style of wine (say, dry red or medium-bodied white) and then some grape varieties that fit that style. In some case, when appropriate, a few regional wines that match the origins of the dish will be included.

Keep in mind that depending on the region, the year and the winemaker, the same grapes may be used in making wines that vary widely, running the gamut from dry and crisp to full-bodied and unctuous. For example, a California Chardonnay may be full-bodied and buttery whereas a French Chablis, also made from the chardonnay grape, is usually drier and refreshingly acidic. This diversity of styles is found in almost all grape varieties in the hands of different vintners. When it comes to selecting wines, consulting a knowledgeable wine merchant is always a good practice.

There is also a section on cocktails and punches to get your party off to a cheery start. In the appendix, look at the section entitled Bar Setup (p.164). From this, you will get an idea of the quantities you will need for your guests.

Shopping Lists

You will be shopping not just for food but also drinks and equipment so it will take organization, list-making, and a few trips. Plan on doing *all* of it before you start your cooking. (Sure, you'll forget stuff but if the bulk of it is out of the way, you're in good shape.) I recommend putting the list on your computer. If you lose it, it is easy to print out a new one and it can be useful for your next party. Before I shop, I print out my menu and make out the shopping list with the recipes in front of me.

Organize the list by place (grocery, liquor store, rental equipment, etc) and then break it down further by category (dairy, vegetables, etc.). Typing the list, you'll find that you can quickly consolidate individual ingredients from different items in your menu.

Food and Drink

When shopping for a large crowd, I look for good buys and reasonable prices. In Paris, I often shop for meat at a local chain store butcher who gives us a reduction in price since the order is often for twenty-five to thirty pounds of meat. Never hesitate to ask for a reduction at a store. Many stores appreciate the large purchase and give a discount.

What are the ethnic stores in your area? Catherine Monnet lives in a section of Paris where there are many middle-Eastern and Greek stores. She buys spices, fruits, vegetables, and staples like twenty-pound bags of rice at a fraction of the cost at a supermarket. Although Catherine likes to bake, sometimes she buys large freshly made trays of baklava, which means the dessert is ready to go. Check out these possibilities in your area.

When you buy liquor or wine by the case, ask your wine merchant if you can bring back unopened bottles. If the bottles have not been chilled, the seller may agree. In this way, you can cover yourself in case of overstocking.

While most ingredients can be bought in advance, there are always the forgotten items, the "I need more of" items, and things such as fresh bread that must be bought the day of the party. So shopping has to be flexible and it really helps to have a go-fer while you're cooking so that when you shriek, "I have to have six lemons *right now*!" your furry friend will spring into action.

At Jim Haynes's Paris atelier, there is a friendly fruit and vegetable stand right outside the front door. What a bonus: not only do they have large quantities, they deliver. This helps with storage since I can delay buying certain things until just before I need them. Maybe you can find a source that delivers in your neighborhood. Your savings of time, energy, and fuel might cover the additional expense of home delivery.

Organize your shopping so that the most perishable items will need the least amount of storage time. For example, arrange to pick up the meat or fish on the day you will cook it. Often, you can order and pay for it in advance and then collect it when you need it. Once cooked, it will take up much less space than in its raw state.

Most fruits, especially strawberries and tomatoes, taste better left out of the refrigerator. Talk over your fruit and vegetable purchases with your produce manager. Ask to have the fruit picked out for you so that it is perfectly ripe for your party.

Serving and Cooking Equipment

What cooking equipment will you need? What you have in your own kitchen will generally work for a party of twenty-five guests. I strongly recommend large chopping boards and sharp knives. Immersion mixers and a food processor or blender are very useful. Microwave ovens perform all sorts of timesaving functions. In the equipment section of this book (see p.165), you will find a table of pots, pans, and baking dishes that will help you determine the sizes you need. One caveat: be sure to measure your oven and stove space to see if extra-large equipment will fit the space.

If you do not have any large pots (and most of us don't) or one hundred plus soup bowls, don't fret. Here are some ways to come up with them:

> **Borrow:** Ask around; many people have platters or a large pot or pan that they would certainly lend you. Neighborhood churches and schools have a lot of kitchen equipment. Do you know anyone who works in a restaurant? They might lend you a really large stockpot or roasting pan.
>
> **Rent:** Glasses and china are just part of the inventory at many rental companies. Large stockpots, skillets, roasting pans, even large outdoor stoves, and grills can be rented.
>
> **Improvise:** Plastic laundry tubs can be pressed into service for mixing, once they are swabbed out. At Jim's, there's a baby's bathtub to mix up the stuffing at Thanksgiving. Its original owner is probably a strapping adult by now. Covering pieces of sturdy

cardboard with heavy-duty foil make good platters for serving breads, cake, and cookies.

Buy: Look for disposable pans for baking and roasting. Foil pans are cheap, disposable, and easy to store. Doubling the pans helps with cooking evenly and provides more stability. "Dollar" discount stores often carry oversized plastic bowls that are useful for mixing, storing, and serving salads. Consider buying equipment you will use again. Restaurant supply stores are mostly open to the public and have surprisingly inexpensive equipment and a huge inventory. As an example, a sixteen-quart stainless steel mixing bowl usually costs less than twenty dollars. Baking sheets are less than ten dollars. Look in your local phone book or go online to find these stores. Bear in mind that much of what is cooked can remain in the pans until serving so it is important to supply yourself with plenty. For serving, consider buying plates, flatware, and glasses. White plates and boxes of sturdy wine glasses can be found for about a dollar each. If you have as few as three parties, having what you need on hand ends up costing less than disposables and you are creating a lot less trash. So look in thrift shops or discount stores for some good values. You can also rent all this equipment. It adds significant expense but often the rental companies will deliver and pick up and you won't have to wash the dishes.

To sum up: whether you beg, borrow, jerry-rig, or buy cheaply, assemble what you need *before* you start the cooking. You'll be able to focus on your preparations if you've got everything you need in advance.

Storage

Storage may seem quite daunting in the average kitchen but it's possible. The kitchen at Jim's has a large refrigerator for Paris but small by U.S. standards and everything gets stored. Here's how to do this in your home:

The first task is to empty your refrigerator completely. Throw out or eat up those five containers of rice, two tacos, and last week's pizza. Take out all the bottled water, soft drinks, and beer. Try to restrict what you must leave (such as milk) on the door of the fridge. Now, take out the shelves. When your produce and meat arrive, you will be able to stack them up. As a precaution, take care to store raw meat and fish on the bottom for faster cooling and to avoid any drips onto other foods.

Packing the refrigerator will be a bit of a balancing act. To fit in as much as possible, eliminate excess packaging before you refrigerate and use closeable plastic bags instead of bulky containers to store foods as they are prepared. You might also put the overflow in a cooler with plenty of ice packs.

Remember, the crush of what seems like an appalling amount of food is just temporary; you're not starting a restaurant. In forty-eight hours, you can return to the happy clutter of fourteen jars of assorted jams, mustard, and hot sauce, the seven ripe knobs of cheese, and the prehistoric jar of sesame tahini you once bought in Morocco.

As food is cooked and stored, label it (masking tape and a marker are ideal). It saves so much time and effort if you can see and read what you have. Trust me: a gallon of frozen soup looks a lot like a gallon of ice cream without a label.

Do not refrigerate your beverages. That is what the ice is for. Beer, soft drinks, and sparkling water can be put on ice thirty minutes before a party starts and will be cold. Put white wine on ice a few bottles at a time, otherwise the labels will come off.

Cooking

To cook for a large group is a different process than cooking for a small number but the basic techniques used in daily cooking are the same. In other words, you don't need to learn *how* to cook a meal of a large size but you do have to envision the process in a new way and that means managing space and allowing enough time.

Before you start to cook, write or print out your menu and copies of the recipes you have chosen. If there are several cooks, everyone will have their copy and won't have to pass cookbooks around. Tape the menu to your wall or cabinet for reference.

For very large gatherings, I write out a prep list of tasks to be completed. It can be as general as "Bake cakes. Make stew. Salad dressing." or more specific but the purpose is to remind me of everything that needs to be completed. The prep list gives you a good sense of what to accomplish first and what to leave for later. If several people are working together, this list helps with assigning various jobs. I tape this on my kitchen wall and cross off each task as it's finished.

Organizing your space

Your work area is important and you need to imagine realistically how you will manage in the space you have. For a very large party, you do not need a large kitchen but you will have to set up or clear a few areas for preparation. If your oven is small, choose menu items that can be cooked in advance or use the stovetop. On the other hand, if your stovetop area is very limited, you might choose to make a salad for a starter and use the oven for your main course. Many foods (Indian dishes are an example) can be served at room temperature, which means you can cook in advance and use a small workspace effectively.

Clear your kitchen counters completely. It is only temporary but stashing the coffee maker, toaster, canisters, and yesterday's mail out of the kitchen will give you space to work. Create more space for chopping and peeling if there are several cooks. A dining room table, suitably covered for protection, will work perfectly. Cover the floor with newspaper or plastic if you have carpeting. You can set up a card table in the garage or work outside at a picnic table. The important thing is not to be crowded and to have a clean surface to work on.

Checking your prep list, set out the tools you will need for cooking such as chopping boards, peelers, graters, and knives. Have a stack of clean dishtowels and a roll of paper towels handy.

Sharpen your knives. The more cooks, the more knives you will need. It's a shame to have willing choppers and peelers available but not the tools to get them to work. If you don't have enough knives, ask your helpers to bring their own. People usually feel more comfortable using their own knives anyway.

Allow enough elbowroom for comfort and safety. Don't share a chopping board; the risk of getting cut is high. Try to manage tasks so that only one person is working at the stove at one time. Reserve an area next to the stove for pans going in and out of the oven. When a dish needs to come out of the oven, you don't want to find yourself with a burning hot pan and no place to set it down.

Read the recipe and assemble all the ingredients.

The recipe instructions will tell you how to cook, assemble, or bake the dish you have chosen. The *recipe list,* however, must be very carefully studied. If it says, "10 pounds onions, chopped" those onions must be chopped *before* you start the cooking. Again, this all takes time. Remember: the menus and recipes in this book are written for either twenty-five or one hundred servings. Plan on cooking the entire recipe for one hundred if your crowd numbers are seventy-five and above; it is always better to have more than less. For numbers between twenty-five and seventy-five, adjust the recipes accordingly.

In this book, you will not find recipes that call for last minute cooking, arranging, or special garnishing. For informal self-catered parties, that type of recipe should be avoided.

Avoid duplicating tasks

Once started, complete each task, such as sautéeing meat, washing lettuce, or peeling potatoes. For example, if you have three dishes that require a total of fifteen pounds of onions, peel and chop *all* of them and then divide what you need for each dish into separate containers.

Seasoning in large quantity

Cooking with large amounts of ingredients is not an exact science and while amounts are usually specific, there are exceptions where you will find 'approximately', 'more if needed' or simply, no quantity listed. Cooking oil is an example where the quantity may be approximate. If sautéeing is called for, the recipe will generally call for heating a small amount and adding more as necessary.

Salt and pepper are usually listed with no quantities. The recipes rarely specify exact amounts of salt and pepper because a great deal depends on the saltiness of the other ingredients and one's own taste. Correctly adjusting the seasoning takes patience and repeated tasting. If a dish is poorly seasoned, under seasoning is usually the culprit as most of us are not used to dealing with very large quantities of food. Think in terms of *tablespoons* of salt rather than teaspoons.

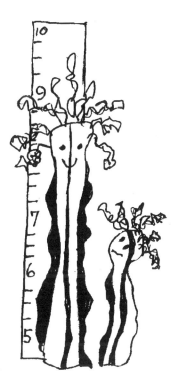

Measuring and equivalents

You will notice that the weights of ingredients, listed in pounds with grams in parentheses may not be exact equivalents. Four or five ounces difference in the amounts won't make a big impact on a dish and rounding up or down facilitates shopping and cooking. If you need exact equivalents, the table in the back of the book is a useful reference (see p.167)

Trust yourself in matters of taste and substitutions: if you like a lot of lemon or prefer thyme to rosemary, make those changes. Changing quantities in baking, however, can be problematic unless you are an experienced dessert maker. To save time and work, you may wish to use frozen vegetables for fresh but be careful to adjust cooking times if you make this kind of substitution.

Set Up and Serving

As with other aspects of cooking for a crowd, envision the serving process in a new way. Make this experience as simple as possible or you will be in a frenzy. The first thing to acknowledge is that when dining with a lot of people in your home (or in the garden or nearby park or the neighbor's barn), you will not be sitting down at the dinner table. You may not be sitting at all.

Buffet or Family Style Dinners

If your guests do not exceed twenty-five or thirty, you can have a seated dinner, using a long table or several smaller ones. In this case, platters of food served family style at the table or a buffet table work well. Dishes and cutlery can be self-serve, arranged on the table with the food or on a side table. A buffet does require attention so that the platters are replenished and the plates cleared. One option is to serve a first course at the table. Have the salad plates or soup bowls ready in advance. When everything is ready and guests are seated, pour the soup or plate the salads, handing them off to one or two servers (or chosen guests) to distribute. You can also have a big bowl and a ladle and pass the bowls. The main course and dessert can be self-serve at the buffet table or from platters passed family style.

If you do plan on serving family style or from a buffet, cook about one and a half times what you think you need. People can be very generous when helping themselves and you want the platters to look full and inviting. So provide ample food and some good bread.

Served Dinners

Feeding a large number of guests is an exercise in traffic management. You want everyone to be fed in a reasonable amount of time without long lines. A practical solution is to serve plates. Portions are controlled and there is no need to replenish or tidy up platters.

For a very large party, I am in favor of a served-plate, three-course meal. Three courses may sound complicated for a crowd but they are by far the easiest to manage. At Jim Haynes's Sunday night dinners, serving separate smaller plates of food is more efficient and appealing than one large, piled-up plate. In terms of timing, the dinner moves smoothly as not all the guests need line up or even arrive at the same time. The Sunday night dinners consist of three courses: salad or soup, a main dish with one or two side dishes served on the same plate, and dessert. Bread is self-serve.

If your space does not allow for serving out of the kitchen, try to find some area where a table can be set up and people can move through a line. Sometimes, setting up a table just outside the kitchen door works well. If the party is outside, set up a serving table as close to the kitchen as possible. You can carry pans from the kitchen to this area as needed. Pots and pans are not a lovely sight but if the emphasis is on getting a tasty meal as quickly and comfortably as possible, this is the way to do it.

Here's how: Have a stack of plates and bowls on one side of a long table. The line will pass down one side of the table with the servers on the opposite side. Store extra plates under the table or within easy reach. At the other end of the table, set out baskets or containers with bread, flatware, napkins, and any garnishes, such as grated cheese or chopped nuts. Guests will help themselves to these items after they've received their food.

For serving in this way, a team of two works best, dividing the serving tasks. Starting with salad or soup, portion out about five bowls at a time. Add to that as people come through the line. After almost everyone has finished their salad or soup, the servers can bring out the main course (saving a few starters for latecomers). For the main course, serve directly from the cooking pots. Guests will let you know if they want smaller portions, vegetables only or any other specific requests but *do not ask* each person what their preferences are. This will slow things down. Most people will pick up a plate as served, and move on.

Wait until you are reasonably certain everyone has had dinner before serving dessert. This will give you a chance to clear a few things away and set out additional flatware and plates. Serve dessert the same way, portioning out bowls or plates. If ice cream is on the menu, soften it several minutes before serving for easier scooping but don't dish up too many bowls at a time.

Don't do more than you need to; if you are serving plates, do not expect to wash dishes at the same time. Whoever is clearing away the plates and glasses should stack them (plastic tubs are good for this) away from serving area.

Setting up a bar

Setting up a space for beer, wine, juice, and water so that guests can serve themselves is a practical and simple way to handle drinks. However, that place cannot be next to the food. Set up a table well away from the food and cover it with a cloth. Underneath the table, stash the beer, water, soft drinks, and some large coolers of ice. Separating the food from the drink cuts down on crowding in one location. If your party is a large one and you are planning on cocktails, wines, or champagne, a bartender is really a good idea. If you not hiring a professional server, plan on two or three reliable volunteers to work in shifts throughout the party. Your helpers will be able to enjoy at least part of the party and avoid burn-out. A good friend, chef Kyle Fehr (who is also an ardent party-giver) says this:

"I find that if I make one special cocktail for the evening, most people will be happy to drink that one. Make a few pitchers of mojitos, margaritas, pomegranate martinis, or whatever and chill them with ice in a shaker. I like to make the first drink for guests, and talk them through it as I'm making it. Then they're on their own."

Another tip:

"You can't have too much ice. I often ask close friends to bring a couple of bags in a cooler. And fill glasses with ice when making drinks, unless you're trying to get everyone trashed."

Clean up

Me? I do it the next day. Or that night. Late. Do whatever makes you most comfortable. And don't forget to return the rentals.

Leftovers need attention too. If you've got a lot, send some home with your guests, keeping just enough so that you and your family won't get sick of it. Speaking of sick, make sure that hot foods have cooled down and stored in small enough containers that they chill quickly in the fridge. This will prevent the growth of bacteria.

Fear of Disaster

As the hour approaches for the start of a party, nerves fray and there's a crackle in the air. Call it pre-bash jitters or stage fright, even Jim Haynes, who's quite a pro, experiences this. The comforting thing to remember is that this state of nerves is momentary.

What really helps is to be ready early. Try to get everything done and get out of the kitchen an hour before people arrive. This not only calms you down, it does your guests a favor. It is hard to have fun when the host appears to be exhausted, struggling out of a stained apron, or dashing around finishing up the cooking. Set the stage: do things ahead, don't get too tired, and be ready. My good friend and super party-giver, Elaine Clayman says this,

"I just stop an hour before my party. I get dressed, I sit down, and I have a drink.

When people get there, everyone has fun."

Fear of disaster or criticism goes deeper than pre-party jitters. Keep in mind that people do not come to parties to be critical. They appreciate your efforts and are delighted to be fed and entertained. And disasters do occur but everyone I've known who has given parties remembers their disasters with humor.

And the stories are incredible (but true): exploding fondues, turkeys escaping their pans, and my favorite: the retrieved pasta. This is what happened: in her open kitchen, with all the guests standing around, the hostess was draining a huge amount of pasta in the sink when it tipped out of the colander and immediately slithered down the garbage disposal. With no time to spare and no extra pasta, she pulled it out of the disposal and onto the platter, saying not a word.

There are also the unexpected or bizarre disasters (the electricity goes out, the toilet backs up when your three-year old flushes a whole apple down it, your cat decides to have her litter in the living room) but these are, believe me, rare. Whatever happens, remember this: *you are with friends*. So, if you've burned the bread or forgotten the beer, chances are someone will run out and get some, or it won't make that much difference.

Never be afraid of cooking for *good* cooks. Even a professional chef will tell you they love to go to parties. Who wants to eat their own food all the time? The pros will come to your party to have a good time not to judge.

A final comment on this subject. Everyone I know who gives great parties says this: invite people you like. Your guests don't have to know each other although it's nice if they know at least one person. One reason Jim's Sunday night dinners are so much fun is that you never know who you will meet. One friend describes her gatherings as 'random' parties. "We don't worry about who's going to get along. We just invite a lot of people we like."

Having Fun

If you've made it this far, you might be overwhelmed by detail but there is still another important aspect about throwing a great party: having fun. Having fun, fortunately, is not something that requires shopping, storing, scheduling, or cooking. It will happen and unexpectedly too. You might look up from peeling onions and see three other faces all streaming with tears. That mountain of apples that everyone is transforming into slices: an occasion for a lot of talk and giggles. As a caterer, I did a lot of prep work at home with a team of fellow cooks. My husband, Paul, at the other end of the house, often remarked how much fun we all had. "Just the shrieks of laughter clued me in that it wasn't just cooking going on." You will be busy during your party but you'll stop and hear laughter, conversation, and happy voices and it will all be worth every second of effort.

So, without further ado, take the plunge, have a party, and have fun.

MENUS

Ivan, meet Odile, Dick this is Camilla, Roland, Diego, Giuseppe, Petra, Wolfgang (He's a chess grand master by the way), Annette, Pablo, Vladimir, Peter, Ljuba, Hassan … Mary, you're not talking to anyone, come over here!

John Calder, quoting Jim Haynes

People are more fun than anything.

Jim Haynes

Some Basic Menu 'Formulas'

The Cold Weather Soup or Stew Menu
(Choose one or two hot soups or a stew
and serve buffet style with a cheese platter,
plenty of assorted breads, and a baked dessert)

A Hot Weather Salad Menu
(Choose three or four salads,
a platter of cold cuts, rolls or cornbread,
and fresh fruit and cookies for dessert)

The Pasta or Chile Dinner
(Choose a baked pasta dish or chile with rice
and serve with a green salad, French bread,
and a fruit dessert)

The Quiche Dinner
(Make two different kinds of quiche,
a tossed salad, bread, and a chocolate dessert)

Seasonal Menus for served dinners or buffets

Spring

These four spring menus range from classic French spring lamb and veal stews to a delicate and subtle Indian feast or Spanish paella. The first menu is a good choice for a three-course meal. Serve the three others either in courses or as a buffet.

I
Asparagus with Pink Onions
Navarin d'Agneau (Spring Lamb Stew)
Cherry Clafoutis

II
Chicken Pasanda in Cashew Sauce
Rice and Raita
Mango, Apple and Apricot Chutney
Sharp Lemon Tart

III
Frisée au Lardons
Blanquette de Veau (Veal Stew)
Parsley Potatoes
Strawberries in Balsamic Vinegar with Pine Nut Cookies

IV
Caesar Salad
Paella
Strawberry Cheesecake

Summer

Seasonal fruits and vegetables highlight these hot weather choices, which can be cooked in advance to keep you and your guests cool at the party. All of these menus are suitable for served courses or for a buffet.

I
Spanakopita (Spinach Cheese Pastries)
Keftedes (Mid-Eastern Meatballs)
Salade Olivier
Taboulé
Melon Salad with Honey, Mint, and Ginger

II
Gaspacho
Moroccan Chicken with Lemons and Olives
Fragrant Couscous
Gajer Halwa (Carrot Halva)

III
Guacamole
Chile Con Carne or Chile Blanco
Cornbread
Cherries and Sliced Watermelon
Seven-Layer Bars

IV
Green Mango Salad
Chicken with Thai Green Curry
Jasmine Rice
Pineapple Sundae with Caramel Sauce

Fall

Hot soups, apple and pear desserts, and some warming main dishes are signs of autumn. Served plates or buffet style will work with these menus.

I
Red Cabbage, Apple, and Walnut Salad
Sweet and Salty Chicken
Chocolate Bread Pudding

II
Sabz Ghost (Lamb in Coconut Milk)
Palak Bhajee (Spicy Spinach)
Masoor Dal (Red Lentils)
Orange Salad with Saffron and Yogurt

III
Tomato and Fennel Soup
Green Le Puy Lentils and Sausages
Fruit Crumble

IV
Provençal Onion and Tomato Tart
Cassoulet (White Bean Stew)
Garlic Bread
Pain d'Epice with Gingered Pears

Winter

Flavorful winter menus feature hearty soups, vegetable salads, and baked desserts with many make-ahead dishes from which to choose.

I
Beet Salad with Shallots, Walnuts, and Parsley
Beef Bourguignon
Puffed Baked Potato Halves
Gâteau au Chocolat à l'Armagnac
(Chocolate Cake with Armagnac)

II
Black Bean Soup
Flat Green Enchilada Casserole
Fiesta Green Salad
Pineapple Upside-Down Cake

III
Blue Cheese, Mushroom, and Endive Salad
Seafood Chowder
Pecan Pie

IV
Grapefruit and Shrimp Salad
Dillkött (Swedish Dill Veal Stew)
Southern Banana Trifle

STARTERS

I didn't know yet that a whole new world was opening up for me, that I was being introduced to a vast, international community of creative, engaged and adventurous people.

Jake Lamar, author, speaking of Jim's Sunday night dinners

APPETIZERS

Catherine Monnet's Guacamole

Avocados in Paris in the 1980's were rare and expensive. Catherine Monnet came up with a way to stretch them and the result was this tasty salsa-like guacamole.

For 25 servings		For 100 servings
½ lb (250 g)	tomatoes	2 lb (1 kg)
8–10	very ripe avocados	30–40
8 Tb	green onions, chopped	½ lb (250 g)
4 Tb	olive oil	1 C (250 ml)
4 Tb (1 lemon)	lemon juice	1 C (4 lemons)
½ C (125 ml)	crème fraîche (see recipe p.151)	2 C (500 ml)
	or sour cream	
	cumin, salt, pepper, Tabasco	
1 bunch	cilantro, chopped	4 bunches

Cut the tomatoes into halves. Working over a bowl or the sink, quickly squeeze each half to release the seeds and juices. Discard the seeds and juices. Dice the tomatoes finely and set aside.

Mash avocados with either a fork or the hands but not in a blender or mixer. Mix in the chopped green onion, olive oil, lemon juice, and crème fraîche. Add generous amounts of cumin, salt, pepper, and Tabasco. Lightly stir in the diced tomatoes and the cilantro and adjust the seasoning just before serving.

Serve with tortilla chips or raw vegetables.

Artichoke Frittata

Not only is this a very good starter that can be prepared ahead, it is also an excellent brunch dish or vegetarian main course.

For 25 servings (about 50 squares)		For 100 servings (about 200 squares)
4 jars	marinated artichoke hearts (6 oz)	16 jars
2 Tb	olive oil	4 Tb
1	onion(s)	4
2 cloves	garlic	8 cloves
8	eggs	32
8 Tb	breadcrumbs	2 C (200 g)
¼ tsp each	black pepper, oregano, dried hot pepper	1 tsp each
1 ½ lb (750 g)	Gruyere or Swiss cheese, shredded	6 lb (2 ½ kg)
4 Tb	parsley, chopped	1 C (125 g)

Drain marinade from the artichoke hearts and reserve ½ cup (for the larger recipe, reserve 1 cup). Heat this liquid with the olive oil and cook the onion and garlic in it until softened.

Combine eggs, breadcrumbs, and seasonings. Fold in cheese and parsley. Chop artichokes coarsely and add them along with the onion mixture. Mix well. Pour mixture into 2 (8-inch) square greased glass pans.

Use 3 (13 x 18-inch) pans for 100 servings and bake 2 pans at a time. Refrigerate the remaining pan until ready to bake.

Bake in a moderate oven (325 F) for about 30 minutes. The top will be browned and puffed slightly. Cool for about 10 minutes before cutting into squares. If prepared ahead, reheat 10 to 12 minutes. Serve hot or at room temperature.

Spanakopita (Spinach Cheese pastries)

These Greek pastries require a little time to prepare but the result is delicious and impressive. If you are working with phyllo leaves for the first time, be sure to buy a few extra sheets until you get the hang of making the pastries. The first sheets may tear or stick but once started, the process goes quickly. You will need a pastry brush or a small clean paintbrush. Serve spanakopita as an appetizer or alongside a main dish. These pastries can be made several days in advance and frozen.

For 25 servings
About 50 pastries

For 100 servings
About 200 pastries

For 25 servings		For 100 servings
2–3 Tb	olive oil, approximately	1/3 C (85 ml)
½ C (125 g)	butter, melted	1 lb (500 g)
2	onions, chopped	8
2 Tb	garlic, finely chopped	½ C (2 heads)
2 lb (1 kg)	frozen spinach, defrosted	8 lb (4 kg)
1 lb (500 g)	Feta cheese, crumbled	4 lb (2 kg)
¾ tsp	nutmeg	3 tsp
½ bunch	parsley, finely chopped	2 bunches
	salt and pepper	
2 lb (1 kg)	phyllo pastry, unthawed	8 lb (4 kg)
(about 30 sheets)		(about 120 sheets)

In a frying pan, sauté the onion and garlic in a few tablespoons of olive oil until softened. Do this in batches, as necessary. Squeeze the spinach in handfuls to remove excess liquid and then chop coarsely. Combine the cooked onion and garlic with the spinach, Feta cheese, parsley, and nutmeg. Add salt and pepper to taste. Mix thoroughly and let cool.

Be sure that the phyllo pastry is completely unthawed. Unroll the pastry and cover it with a piece of plastic or waxed paper followed by a damp dishcloth to keep from drying out while working. On a clean, dry surface, lay one sheet flat and brush lightly with butter. Top with the second sheet, brush with butter, and top with the third sheet. Cut into 5 strips cross-wise. Place a rounded tablespoon of the spinach mixture at the top of each strip. Fold over forming a triangle and continue to fold up like a flag. Brush each triangle with more butter. Proceed with all the phyllo sheets in the same fashion, placing the triangles 1 inch apart on large baking sheets, lined with parchment paper.

Bake pastries in a moderate oven (350 F) for 20 to 30 minutes, or until golden brown. Serve warm or at room temperature. To freeze, arrange the prepared triangles in single layers in closable plastic bags or wrapped in plastic. Bake the triangles unthawed in the same manner as above.

Spicy Peanut Dip with Fresh Vegetables

"If there's one recipe that I get asked for all time, it's this spicy peanut dip." This is a favorite from Mary Bartlett and a great make-ahead choice. The secret is using peanuts rather than peanut butter. The crudités can be prepared early on the day of the party and packaged in separate plastic bags or containers. Putting together a beautiful platter takes just a few minutes.

For 25 servings		For 100 servings
2 C (250 g)	peanuts	2 lb (1 kg)
4 Tb	tea, cooled	1 C (250 ml)
4 Tb	red wine vinegar	1 C (250 ml)
½ C (125 ml)	soy sauce	2 C (500 ml)
1 tsp	sesame oil	4 tsp
1 C (250 ml)	mayonnaise	1 qt (1 L)
2 tsp	Dijon mustard	2 Tb
1 Tb	chili garlic sauce (or more to taste)	4 Tb

Using a food processor or blender, grind the peanuts finely. For the larger recipe, do this in batches. Add everything else and blend until smooth. Refrigerate until ready to serve. The sauce will become quite thick. Thin it with water or tea.

This dip can be made several days in advance.

Fresh Vegetables (or Crudités)

The following list is simply a general guide. Add or omit any vegetable but bear in mind, that you need enough to make a platter look full and inviting even though you may have leftovers. In season, asparagus and green beans make lovely additions but they are much better cooked and chilled rather than served raw. Serve the peanut dip on the platter in a bowl or in a shell made out of red cabbage leaves.

For 25 servings		For 100 servings
1 each	red, yellow, and green pepper	4 each
1	English cucumber	4
2	small green zucchinis	6
2	small yellow squash	6
3	carrots	10
1 bunch	radishes, trimmed	2 bunches
1 handful	pea pods	¼ lb (125 g)
½ lb (250 g)	broccoli, in florets	1 head
½ lb (250 g)	cauliflower, in florets	1 head
	Optional:	
1 lb (500 g)	asparagus	2 lbs (1 kg)
1 lb (500 g)	green beans, trimmed	2 lbs (1 kg)
1	red cabbage (to make a 'bowl')	1
1 bunch	parsley or other fresh herbs	2 bunches

Prepare the peppers, cucumber, squash, and carrots by slicing each into julienne strips or rounds or shapes, large enough for dipping but not too thin that they will break. The pea pods taste better if they are blanched briefly in boiling water, then put in ice water and dried well.

Package each vegetable separately either in containers or closeable bags and refrigerate. If using asparagus, snap off the woody ends and boil in salted water until just done. Plunge into ice water, drain, wrap in paper towels and a plastic bag, and refrigerate. Follow the same method for green beans.

At serving time, arrange the vegetables in groups on a platter, alternating colors, and shapes. Make a 'bowl' from the sturdy leaves of a red cabbage and pour in the peanut dip or use a glass bowl. If the vegetables are covered with damp paper towels, they can sit for about ½ hour before serving. Decorate the platter with small bunches of fresh herbs, if desired.

For the larger recipe, you may set up one platter as described above and refill with vegetables as needed. Alternatively, make up two platters in advance. Set out one at a time. When the first gets low on vegetables, it is easy to replace it with the reserved platter.

SOUPS

To make soup in large quantity, you will need some very large stockpots or divide the ingredients between two smaller ones. See the equipment list in the appendix section (p.165) for appropriate pot sizes. Most soups can be made ahead with any garnish reserved separately. If you do make soup ahead, it must be cooled down before refrigerating to avoid spoilage. To speed up the cooling of large quantities of soup, especially on hot days, put the whole pot in a sink full of ice water. Stir every few minutes to cool down quickly. When lukewarm, refrigerate, uncovered. Stir occasionally until completely cool and then, cover.

Alladine's Zucchini Soup

Alladine LaCroix is a writer in Paris and a good friend of Jim. She furnished this very easy recipe, which uses simple and inexpensive ingredients. The richness of the soup depends on whether you use cream or milk. Serve hot or cold.

For 25 servings		For 100 servings
25 medium	zucchinis, quartered	33 lb (15 kg)
1 lb (500 g)	"Vache qui Rit" cheese (Laughing cow)	4 lb (2 kg)
2 C (500 ml)	whole milk or cream	2 qt (2 L)
	salt and pepper	
2 bunches	chives, chopped	8 bunches

Cook the zucchini in boiling, salted water until tender, about 10 minutes. Drain, reserving the liquid. Working in batches, purée the zucchini in a blender with the cheese, adding cooking liquid as necessary. Add salt and pepper to taste, and add milk or cream to desired consistency. Serve cold or hot with chopped chives on top.

Black bean soup with cumin and cilantro

This black bean soup is without meat, which always pleases vegetarians in the crowd. In France, spicy foods are not very well received and so the hot peppers are served on the side at Jim's parties.

For 25 servings		For 100 servings
1 ¾ lb (750 g)	dried black beans	7 lb (3 kg)
4 Tb	olive oil	1 C (250 ml)
1 lb (500 g)	onions, diced	4 lb (2 kg)
½ lb (250 g)	carrots, diced	2 lb (1 kg)
½ lb (250 g)	celery, diced	2 lb (1 kg)
¼ C (1 head)	garlic, chopped	1 C (4 heads)
2 Tb	ground cumin	8 Tb
2 Tb	ground coriander	8 Tb
1 C (250 ml)	Port	1 bottle (750 ml)
½ bunch	cilantro, chopped	2 bunches
1 C (250 ml)	crème fraîche (see recipe p.151)	1 qt (1 L)
	or sour cream	
	salt and pepper	
3	limes	10
	Bottled hot sauce	
	Or	
	1 large can of jalapenos, chopped	

Soak beans several hours or overnight. Drain and put in a heavy pot, adding water to cover by 2 inches. Bring to a boil. Reduce heat, cover, and simmer until beans are tender, stirring occasionally, about 2 ½ hours, adding more water if necessary.

While the beans are cooking, heat oil in a large pot over medium-high heat. Sauté onions, carrots, celery, and garlic until soft but not browned. Add to the cooked beans along with the spices.

Season with salt and pepper. For a smooth soup, purée the beans using an immersion mixer or a blender. If not serving immediately, cool down and refrigerate. This can be made a few days in advance.

Reheat, stirring, and add the port wine and half of the cilantro. Thin the soup with water if it is too thick. Bring just to the boil and simmer about 10 minutes. Add the cream. Check the seasoning, adding more salt if necessary. Serve with separate bowls of lime wedges, the remaining cilantro, and jalapenos or hot sauce.

Tomato and Fennel Soup

Pernod is essential for the flavor in this soup but Herbsaint, a New Orleans anise liqueur is less expensive and a good substitute. This soup is a crowd pleaser.

For 25 servings		For 100 servings
4 oz (125 g)	butter, unsalted	1 lb (500 g)
1 lb (500 g)	onions, chopped	4 lb (2 kg)
½ lb (250 g)	carrots, chopped	2 lb (1 kg)
1 ½ lb (750 g)	fennel, chopped	6 lb (3 kg)
¾ C (187 ml)	Pernod or other anise liquor	1 bottle (750ml)
3 cans	tomatoes (29 oz/765g)	12 cans
1 qt (1 L)	chicken or vegetable broth	4 qt (4 L)
5 sprigs	tarragon	2 bunches
5 sprigs	parsley	2 bunches
2 C (500 ml)	crème fraîche (see recipe p.151) or cream	2 qt (2 L)
1 Tb	salt	4 Tb

Melt the butter in a very large pot and add the onions, carrots, and fennel, stirring well. Cover and cook over medium heat stirring occasionally until the vegetables are completely softened. This could take up to 30 minutes for the larger amount.

Add the tomatoes and enough broth to fill the pot ¾ full. Tie the tarragon and parsley with string into bunches. Add these and the Pernod to the soup. Bring to a boil and then simmer over low heat for 15 minutes. Remove the tarragon and parsley. Taste and add salt as necessary.

Purée the soup in a blender or food processor or use an immersion blender. The soup can be made in advance to this point. Cool it down and refrigerate for up to 2 days.

Before serving, return the soup to a simmer and add the crème fraîche. If the soup is too thick, thin it with more broth or water. Adjust the seasoning.

Pumpkin Soup

A favorite autumn starter, this pumpkin soup has a rich, velvety texture. Be careful not to boil it once the milk is added or it will curdle. If you have time, using fresh pumpkin makes a splendid soup. Good served with croutons.

For 25 servings		For 100 servings
5 lb (2 ½ kg)	fresh pumpkin	20 lb (9 kg)
	Or	
3 cans	canned pumpkin, (16 oz/500 g)	12 cans
1 ½ lb (700 g)	onions, chopped	6 lb (2 ½ kg)
5 Tb	butter	¾ lb (300 g)
2 ½ C (625 ml)	whole milk	2 ½ qt (2 ½ L)
1 ½ qt (1 ½ L)	chicken broth	5 qt (5 L)
5 tsp	nutmeg	4 Tb
	salt and pepper	
½ C (125 ml)	crème fraîche (see recipe p.151)	2 C (500 ml)
	or heavy cream	
	Optional garnish:	
1 C (250 ml)	crème fraîche (or heavy cream)	1 qt (1 L)
8 oz (250 g)	croutons (see recipe p.44)	2 lb (1 kg)

If using fresh pumpkin, heat the oven to 350 F. Cut the pumpkins into large sections and bake on sheet pans for 45 minutes to 1 hour until the pumpkin is soft. Add a little water to the pans to keep the pumpkin pieces from drying out. Cool and scrape, discarding the seeds and strings. Scoop out the flesh and set aside. Discard the rinds.

Heat the butter in very large pot over medium-high heat. Add the onions and sauté until softened but not browned. Add the pumpkin to the onions, stirring gently and then add milk, broth, nutmeg, salt, and pepper. Bring to simmering point and cook for 30 minutes. Do not boil.

Purée the mixture in batches using an immersion mixer or a blender. Taste for seasoning, adding more salt, pepper, and nutmeg as desired. If not serving immediately, cool down and refrigerate.

Re-heat when needed and stir in the crème fraîche. For a garnish, provide bowls of additional crème fraîche and croutons.

Gazpacho

There are many variations of this Spanish summer soup. Some are creamy, others chunky, some very liquid, like drinking V8 juice, others very thick. Adding some of the cucumbers and peppers separately gives this one a nice texture. Homemade croutons or garlic toasts are a terrific garnish.

For 25 servings		For 100 servings
2	green peppers	8
3	English cucumbers	12
6 lb (2 ½ kg)	tomatoes, peeled* and chopped	24 lb (10 kg)
5 cloves	garlic	20 cloves
2	red peppers, chopped	8
1 lb (500 g)	onions, chopped	4 lb (2 kg)
6 C (1 ½ L)	tomato juice	6 qt (6 L)
5 slices	white bread, crusts removed	20 slices
4 Tb	vinegar	1 C (250 ml)
8 Tb	olive oil	2 C (500 ml)
1 bunch	parsley, finely chopped	4 bunches
	salt, pepper, Tabasco	
	Optional:	
8 oz (250 g)	croutons (see recipe p.44)	2 lb (1 kg)
	or garlic toasts (see recipe p.103)	

Peel and finely chop the green peppers and half of the cucumbers and set aside. Coarsely chop the remaining cucumbers.

In as many batches as necessary, using a food processor or blender, combine the tomatoes, garlic, red peppers, onions, tomato juice, vinegar, olive oil, bread slices, and coarsely chopped cucumbers. Blend until smooth. Stir in the reserved cucumber, green pepper, and parsley. Add salt, pepper, and Tabasco to taste.

Chill the mixture at least 2 hours or overnight. Serve in bowls, topped with croutons or a garlic toast, if desired.

*You may balk at peeling tomatoes but your soup will have a better texture without the tomato skins. The process goes very quickly once you have set up a large bowl of ice water and have a pan of boiling water on the stove. With a very sharp knife, (a small serrated one is best), lightly cut an X on the blossom end of the tomato. Put three or four tomatoes at one time into the boiling water and count to 10. Transfer the tomatoes with a slotted spoon into the ice water. Slip off the skins. If they do not come off easily, put them back in the boiling water a few seconds longer.

Jessie's Thai-way Soup (Vegetarian)

On a visit to Paris, Jessica Buck made a soup that was a hit on a warm June evening at Jim's. "Real Thai soup is not puréed," the Portland, Oregon writer explained, "But I hated to strain out the vegetables so I came up with this version." The seasoning at the end is most important. The lime juice creates a lovely, fresh taste, so do not hesitate to be generous with this ingredient.

For 25 servings		For 100 servings
5 or 6 cubes	vegetable bouillon	20–25 cubes
5 stalks	lemon grass	20 stalks
1 can	tomatoes, (29 oz/765g)	4 cans
½ lb (250 g)	mushrooms, coarsely chopped	2 lb (1 kg)
1 lb (500 g)	potatoes, peeled and cubed	4 lb (2 kg)
1 lb (500 g)	leeks, white and pale green parts, sliced	4 lb (2 kg)
1 (6-inch) piece	ginger, peeled and grated	4 (6-inch) pieces
½ C (2 heads)	garlic, chopped	2 C (8 heads)
Juice of 5	limes	Juice of 15 to 20
2 cans	coconut milk, (5.6 oz), unsweetened	8 cans
1 large bunch	cilantro, chopped	4 bunches
	hot chile sauce or hot peppers	

For 25 servings, fill an 8-quart pot 1/3 full of water and bring to a boil. For the larger recipe, use a 32-quart (liter) pot. Add enough bouillon cubes to the boiling water to make a broth that is not too strongly flavored.

With the flat of a large knife or a rolling pin, crush the ends of the lemon grass stalks. Add half of the stalks to the broth and simmer for 10 minutes. Remove the lemon grass and discard. Add the tomatoes, mushrooms, potatoes, leeks, half of the ginger, and half of the garlic. Bring to a boil and then simmer until all the vegetables are cooked and tender (about 10 to 15 minutes). This step may take longer for the large recipe. Let cool about 20 minutes.

Purée in batches using an immersion wand, blender, or food processor and return to the pot. Add the lime juice and coconut milk, half of the chopped cilantro, and the remaining lemon grass. After tasting, add enough of the remaining garlic and ginger to enhance the taste. Reheat and simmer a few minutes.

Before serving, remove the lemon grass and discard. Taste for seasoning, adding hot sauce if desired. Serve hot or cold with the remaining chopped cilantro as well as additional hot sauce on the side.

SALADS

Beet Salad with Shallots, Walnuts, and Parsley

In the local markets in Paris, beets are sold cooked, which is a great timesaver. Canned or vacuum-packed beets can be substituted for fresh ones in this salad but some flavor is certainly sacrificed so if you have the time, follow the method for cooking raw beets. The vinaigrette is tart and peppery to offset a bit of the sweetness of the beets.

For 25 servings		For 100 servings
5 lb (2 ½ kg)	beets, cooked and peeled*	20 lb (8 kg)
1 lb (500 g)	walnuts, toasted briefly	4 lb (2 kg)
12 oz (375 g)	shallots, minced	3 lb (1 ½ kg)
1 bunch	parsley, finely chopped	4 bunches

Chop beets into bite sized pieces and place in a large bowl. Chop the walnuts coarsely. Make the vinaigrette.

If the salad is to be served later, store all of the ingredients in separate closed containers, (closeable plastic bags are handy), in the refrigerator.

To serve: Beat the vinaigrette to emulsify and add to the remaining ingredients in a large bowl. Toss lightly but thoroughly. Serve in small bowls or plates.

*To cook raw beets in quantity:

Thoroughly scrub beets, having first cut off the greens but leaving about an inch of stalk at the top. Place the beets in 1 or 2 baking or roasting pans, packing them in one layer. Drizzle generously with olive oil and season with salt and pepper. With your hands, roll the beets in the oil and seasonings so all sides are covered. Cover the pans tightly with foil and bake in a moderately hot oven (375 F) for 1 hour. Check for tenderness by piercing with a knife. Beets cook slowly and may need more time. Cool and peel, using rubber gloves to keep your hands from staining.

Vinaigrette

1 Tb	garlic, finely chopped	4 Tb
¾ C (187 ml)	red wine vinegar	3 C (750 ml)
1 ½ C (375 ml)	olive oil	1 ½ qt (1 ½ L)
1 ½ tsp	salt	2 Tb
1 ½ tsp	pepper	2 Tb

Place the vinegar, garlic, salt, and pepper in a large bowl and whisk in the olive oil in a steady stream. Store in a closed container until ready to serve.

Blue cheese, mushroom, and endive salad

In France, endives are abundant and inexpensive. They appear in a variety of salads, cooked as a vegetable or even as a popular main dish with ham and cheese. This winter salad has a fresh crisp texture and the slight bitterness particular to endives.

For 25 servings		For 100 servings
3 lb (1 ½ kg)	endives	12 lb (5 kg)
1 lb (500 g)	mushrooms	4 lb (2 kg)
½ lb (250 g)	Roquefort or blue cheese, crumbled	2 lb (1 kg)
	Basic I Vinaigrette (see recipe p.53)	

Chop endives into 1-inch pieces, discarding the stem ends. Slice the mushrooms. Toss endives and mushrooms with the vinaigrette and season with salt and pepper. Gently, mix in the Roquefort or blue cheese and serve.

Caesar Salad

Everyone loves this salad and comes back for seconds. Homemade croutons and genuine Parmesan cheese really make this salad exceptional. Without the anchovies, the salad is not a Caesar but in this recipe, they are optional in case your crowd has objections.

For 25 servings		For 100 servings
3 lb (1 ½ kg)	romaine lettuce	12 lb (5 kg)
10 oz (300 g)	Parmesan, grated	2 ½ lb (1 ¼ kg)
½ lb (250 g)	croutons (see recipe p.44)	2 lb (1 kg)
8	eggs, hard boiled, chopped	36
	Optional:	
4 oz (125 g)	canned anchovies, drained	1 lb (500g)

Caesar Dressing

½ C (2 lemons)	lemon juice	2 C (8 lemons)
4 Tb	mustard	1 C (250 ml)
2 Tb	garlic, finely chopped	½ C (2 heads)
2 Tb	Worcestershire Sauce	½ C (125 ml)
1 C (250 ml)	olive oil	1 qt (1 L)
	salt and pepper	

Tear the romaine lettuce leaves into bite-sized pieces. Place in a large bowl topped with Parmesan cheese, eggs, and croutons. Combine all the ingredients for the dressing, add to the salad, and toss. Add the anchovies, left whole or chopped, as desired.

Serve immediately.

Croutons

The trick here is not to leave the stove for an instant for they burn very easily.

For 25 servings   For 100 servings

1	baguette(s)	4
1 C (250 ml)	olive oil	1 qt (L)
1	garlic clove(s), whole, smashed	4
	salt and pepper	

Cut the baguettes into slices and then cubes of approximately the same size. Heat about ¼ of the oil in a large skillet until hot but not smoking. Add a piece of garlic to the oil as it heats up and then discard before it browns.

Working in batches, add about ¼ of the bread cubes, tossing to cover with the oil. Continue to stir over moderate heat, transferring them to baking sheets covered with paper toweling as they begin to brown. Season immediately with salt and pepper.

Continue in this fashion, heating additional oil and garlic until all the croutons have been sautéed and seasoned.

When cool, store in airtight containers or closeable plastic bags. If necessary, heat the croutons in a warm oven (200 F) for a few minutes to crisp. May be made several days in advance.

"Fiesta" Salad

Easy and colorful, this salad can be served as a first course or on the same plate as a main course such as chili con carne. The prepared ingredients can be stored in separate, closeable plastic bags or covered bowls a day in advance of serving.

For 25 servings		For 100 servings
3 lb (1 ½ kg)	salad greens	12 lb (5 kg)
5	red peppers, sliced in rings	20
2 lb (1 kg)	canned corn, drained	8 lb (4 kg)
¾ lb (750 g)	black olives, pitted, and sliced	3 lb (1 ½ kg)
	Basic II, Lemon, or Orange-Cumin Vinaigrette (see recipes pp. 54 and 55)	
	salt and pepper	

Toss all the salad ingredients together just before serving. Mix in the dressing and add salt and pepper to taste.

Frisée aux Lardons

This traditional French salad is often served as a first course in Paris bistros. Thickly cut bacon pieces, called 'lardons' are mixed with frisée, a crisp and rather bitter lettuce. Dandelion greens or escarole may be substituted for frisée.

For 25 servings   For 100 servings

4 lb (2 kg)	frisée lettuce	16 lb (7 kg)
1 ½ lb (750 g)	bacon, thickly sliced	6 lb (2 ½ kg)
	salt and pepper	
	Basic II Vinaigrette (see recipe p.54)	

Sauté the bacon until crisp and drain on paper towels. Crumble or cut into small pieces. Set aside.

Wash and dry the frisée. Prepare the vinaigrette.

At serving time, re-crisp the bacon briefly in the microwave. Toss the frisée and the bacon with enough vinaigrette to coat well. Add salt and pepper to taste but take care not to overseason, as the bacon may be quite salty.

Grapefruit, Shrimp and Pecan Salad

Guests at Jim's dinners in Paris rave about this popular winter appetizer and your guests will too. Peeling the grapefruit takes some time but may be done ahead. Here's a handy trick to combat the bland character of frozen shrimp: season it separately before mixing with the other ingredients. Be sure to add some nuts for "crunch" to complete this salad.

For 25 servings		For 100 servings
8	grapefruit	24
2 lb (1 kg)	small shrimp, peeled	8 lb (4 kg)
1	lemon(s)	4
4 Tb	olive oil	1 C (250 ml)
2 lb (1 kg)	mixed salad greens	8 lb (4 kg)
	Lemon Vinaigrette (see recipe p.54)	
½ lb (250 g)	toasted almonds or pecans	2 lb (1 kg)

Prepare the grapefruit by removing all the peel and the white pith from each. Cut into sections or thick slices and place in a large bowl. Refrigerate until serving time.

An hour before serving, place all the shrimp in a bowl and season generously with lemon juice, olive oil, salt and pepper. Mix well, cover the bowl, and refrigerate.

To serve the salad, combine the ingredients in a large bowl a batch at a time in the following manner: place about ¼ of the greens in the bowl with some of the vinaigrette and toss. Fold in about ¼ of the grapefruit sections and ¼ of the shrimp. Serve in small bowls. For each serving, sprinkle with about 1 tablespoon of toasted nuts. Continue to combine the ingredients in batches.

Green Salad with Fennel, Sun-Dried Tomatoes, and Pine Nuts

This simple all-season salad goes nicely with any main dish. The fennel and pine nuts add crunch, the fresh Parmesan special flavor, and the sun dried tomatoes a little color and sweetness.

For 25 servings		For 100 servings
½ lb (250 g)	pine nuts	2 ½ lb (1 kg)
5	large fennel bulbs, thinly sliced	20
3 lb (1 ½ kg)	salad greens	12 lb (5 kg)
12 oz (375 g)	Parmesan, shaved	3 lb (1 ½ kg)
½ lb (250 g)	sun-dried tomatoes, thinly sliced	2 lb (1 kg)
	olive oil	
	salt and pepper	
	Basic II or Orange Cumin Vinaigrette	
	(see recipes pp. 54 and 55)	

Heat a few tablespoons of olive oil in a frying pan and sauté the pine nuts until they are very light brown. Do this in batches, if necessary. Watch carefully as they burn easily. Drain on paper towels and season with salt. When cool, store in a covered container or plastic bag. This may be done a few days in advance.

Refrigerate the sliced fennel in a bowl with cold water to cover to avoid browning. Prepare a 'kit' with the remaining salad items, placing them in separate bowls or closeable plastic bags. Refrigerate.

At serving time, mix together the salad greens, fennel, and sun-dried tomatoes. Toss together with dressing and season with salt and pepper.

Serve in small bowls and sprinkle with pine nuts and Parmesan.

Greek Salad

Colorful, festive and easy for a large crowd. This salad can be completely prepared in advance and tossed at serving time. A storage tip: large bowls of salad can be stacked in the refrigerator using baking sheets or trays to separate and balance them.

For 25 servings		For 100 servings
2 lb (1 kg)	salad greens	8 lb (4 kg)
2	cucumbers, sliced	8
3 lb (1 ½ kg)	tomatoes, cut in wedges	12 lb (5 kg)
1 lb (500 g)	red onions, thinly sliced	4 lb (2 kg)
2 lb (1 kg)	green peppers, thinly sliced	8 lb (4 kg)
1 lb (500 g)	black Greek olives, pitted	4 lb (2 kg)
2 lb (1 kg)	Feta cheese, crumbled	8 lb (4 kg)
	Basic I or II Vinaigrette (see recipes pp. 53 and 54)	

Starting with salad greens, layer all the ingredients in large bowls. Cover well and refrigerate. This can be done one day in advance.

Toss together all the ingredients with the dressing just before serving.

Green Mango Salad

This salad makes a delightful appetizer or side dish with a spicy curry. The job of grating the mangoes can be speeded up a bit if you have a food processor. The ingredients can be prepared in the morning and put together at serving time.

For 25 servings		For 100 servings
4	large firm mangoes	16
1 C	unsweetened coconut	4 C
2 ½ lbs (1 kg)	bean sprouts	10 lb (5 kg)
1 bunch	basil	4 bunches
2 bunches	scallions	8 bunches
½ C (125 ml)	fish sauce	2 C (500 ml)
½ C (125 ml)	lime juice	2 C (500 ml)
4 Tb	brown sugar	1 C (200 g)
1–2 Tb	Thai chili sauce or chili garlic sauce	4–8 Tb

Toast the coconut in a dry frying pan, taking care as it burns easily. Let cool, cover and set aside.

Peel the mangos and grate or julienne finely. Refrigerate covered. Rinse the bean sprouts quickly in water, drain, and refrigerate.

Mix the fish sauce, lime juice, sugar, and chili sauce for the dressing and set aside.

To serve, combine the mango with the basil, scallions, bean sprouts, coconut, and the dressing, mixing gently.

Red cabbage, apple and walnut salad

Shredding cabbage and cutting apples takes some time but this salad is an especially good fall or winter choice. It is loaded with flavor, inexpensive to make, and healthy to boot. Once the ingredients are prepared, it is simple to put together and toss up to an hour before serving. Even with lemon juice, the cut apples will discolor somewhat but once the salad is dressed, they will look fine. If available, hazelnuts (filberts) are a good alternative to walnuts.

For 25 servings		For 100 servings
2 lb (1 kg)	tart, firm apples	8 lb (4 kg)
Juice of 1	lemon(s)	Juice of 4
3 lb (1 ½ kg)	red cabbage	12 lb (5 kg)
¾ lb (750 g)	walnuts, chopped	3 lb (1 ½ kg)

Poppy (or Caraway) seed Vinaigrette

4 Tb	mustard	1 C (250 ml)
¾ C (187 ml)	vinegar	3 C (750 ml)
2 C (500 ml)	olive oil	2 qt (2 L)
1 C (250 ml)	mayonnaise	1 qt (1 L)
½ C (125 ml)	honey	2 C (500 ml)
1 Tb	poppy or caraway seeds	4 oz (125 g)
	salt, pepper	

Peel and core the apples and cut into either small chunks or slices. Toss with lemon juice to discourage browning.

Shred the cabbage by either slicing finely or using a slicer.

Mix all the ingredients for the vinaigrette and toss with the cabbage, apples, and walnuts.

Taboulé

This recipe comes from Jim's friend, Dominique Ferry. "A long time ago, a friend welcomed me to Paris, by inviting me out to dinner. Jim, sitting at another table, invited us for a coffee and soon after, I found my way to his atelier in the rue Tombe-Issoire. Jim welcomed so many sweet earthlings: strange characters, international kids, and true friends. At first, the dinners involved a few friends but suddenly it was like forty people; then guests started volunteering and there was some wild cooking at that time."

For 25 servings		For 100 servings
3 lb (1 ½ kg)	couscous or bulgar	12 lb (5 kg)
1 ½ C (6 lemons)	lemon juice	1 ½ qt (24 lemons)
2 lb (1 kg)	tomatoes, diced	8 lb (4 kg)
1 lb (500 g)	onions, finely chopped	4 lb (2 kg)
3 cloves	garlic	12 cloves
2	English cucumbers, diced	8
3	green peppers, finely chopped	12
2 bunches	parsley, finely chopped	8 bunches
	salt	
	paprika	
2 C (500 ml)	olive oil	2 qt (2 L)
2 C (500 ml)	tomato juice	2 qt (2 L)
8 bunches	mint, leaves only	30 bunches

Divide the couscous between 2 very large bowls and stir in the lemon juice. The lemon juice "cooks" the couscous.

Mix the tomatoes, onions, garlic, cucumbers, peppers, and parsley into the couscous. Add salt and paprika to taste and the olive oil. If the couscous seems dry, add tomato juice. Chop the mint and stir in.

Let the couscous rest a minimum of 2 hours before serving.

VINAIGRETTES

Even the fanciest bottled dressings do not measure up to homemade. Here are five vinaigrettes that may be made several days in advance and kept in the refrigerator. Simply shake or stir vigorously to re-combine.

Basic I Vinaigrette

This is the sharpest vinaigrette. Vinegars vary greatly in acidity so be sure to taste and add more olive oil if the sharpness overpowers you.

For 25 servings		For 100 servings
2 Tb	Dijon mustard	8 Tb
4 Tb	red wine vinegar	1 C (250 ml)
¾ C (187 ml)	olive oil	3 C (750 ml)
1 tsp	salt	4 tsp
¼ tsp	pepper	1 tsp

In a medium-sized bowl, whisk together the mustard and vinegar. Add the oil in a slow steady stream, whisking constantly until all the oil is added and the mixture is completely emulsified. Add salt and pepper, taste, adding more seasoning if necessary.

Basic II Vinaigrette

Adding some balsamic vinegar makes this vinaigrette slightly smoother and sweeter.

For 25 servings		For 100 servings
2 Tb	Dijon mustard	8 Tb
2 Tb	balsamic vinegar	½ C (125 ml)
2 Tb	red wine vinegar	½ C (125 ml)
¾ C (187 ml)	olive oil	3 C (750 ml)
1 tsp	salt	4 tsp
¼ tsp	pepper	1 tsp

In a medium-sized bowl, whisk together the mustard and both vinegars. Add the oil in a slow steady stream, whisking constantly until all the oil is added and the mixture is completely emulsified. Add salt and pepper to taste.

Lemon Vinaigrette

There is no substitute for fresh juice in this very simple vinaigrette.

For 25 servings		For 100 servings
4 Tb (1–2 lemons)	lemon juice	1 C (4–6 lemons)
1 tsp	salt	4 tsp
¼ tsp	pepper	1 tsp
¾ C (187 ml)	olive oil	3 C (750 ml)
	Optional:	
½ bunch	mixed fresh herbs, finely chopped (parsley, tarragon, chives, or chervil)	2 bunches

In a medium-sized bowl, combine the lemon juice, salt, and pepper. Add the oil in a slow steady stream, whisking constantly until all the oil is added. Taste and add more seasoning, as necessary. If using fresh herbs, add them shortly before serving or they will turn yellow.

Orange Cumin Vinaigrette

Good with robust salads such as spinach, tuna, or black bean.

½ C (125 ml)	orange juice	2 C (500 ml)
2 tsp	cumin	2 ½ Tb
1 small clove	garlic, minced	2 cloves
4 Tb	rice wine or white wine vinegar	1 C (250 ml)
½ C (125 ml)	canola or safflower oil	2 C (500 ml)
	salt, pepper	

Prepare the vinaigrette by combining the juice, vinegar, and seasonings. Whisking steadily, add the oil in a steady stream. Taste for seasoning, adding salt and pepper.

Balsamic Vinaigrette

Balsamic vinaigrette need not be lackluster. The quality and cost of the vinegar varies wildly from the rich, aged variety to a thinner less expensive variety. Using modestly priced vinegar, this recipe makes very good balsamic vinaigrette. The shallots, touch of sugar and black pepper are the secret.

For 25 servings		For 100 servings
4 Tb	balsamic vinegar	1 C (250 ml)
1 ½ tsp	brown sugar	2 Tb
1 tsp (scant)	pepper	1 Tb
¾ C (187 ml)	olive oil	3 C (750 ml)
4 Tb	shallots, finely chopped	½ lb (250 g)
1 tsp	salt	4 tsp

Prepare the vinaigrette by combining the vinegar, sugar, and pepper. Whisking steadily, add the oil in a steady stream. Add the shallots at the end and taste carefully, adding the salt.

MAIN DISHES

Quand j'entends les voix et les éclats de rire, je suis hereuse parce que la joie de se rencontrer et de vivre quelques heures agréables—c'est la vie.

(When I hear people's voices, and their sudden bursts of laughter, I am happy. Happy because the joy of meeting people and spending a few pleasant hours with them—that is what life is all about.)

Madame Paupèrt, Jim's upstairs neighbor

I've always been optimistic and incredibly happy.

Jim Haynes

FISH AND SHELLFISH

Paella

Paella is not inexpensive to make but it shouts, "Party!" Colin Gravois, a native of Vacherie, Louisiana and a good friend of Jim Haynes was the inspiration for the following recipe, which he makes outside over a fire. Having prepared this dish many times for a huge crowd, Catherine Monnet developed a method using the oven rather than the traditional paella pan. Allow plenty of time for sautéeing the vegetables, meats, and seafood and be sure to have several very large pots and bowls for the cooking process.

For 25 servings		For 100 servings
1 ¼ tsp	saffron threads	5 tsp
1 C (250 ml)	olive oil, approximately	1 qt (1 L)
1 ½ lb (750 g)	onions, chopped	6 lb (3 kg)
3	red peppers, chopped	12
3	green peppers, chopped	12
2 Tb	garlic, finely chopped	½ C (2 heads)
3 lb (1 ½ kg)	rice	12 lb (5 kg)
4 oz (125 g)	peas, frozen	1 lb (500 g)
1 bunch	parsley, finely chopped	4 bunches

2–3 cans	tomatoes, canned (29 oz/765g)	10 cans
2 Tb	paprika	8 Tb
2 Tb	oregano	8 Tb
	salt and pepper	
1 lb (500 g)	chorizo, chopped	4 lb (2 kg)
½ lb (500 g)	calamari, sliced	2 lb (1 kg)
2 lb (1 kg)	shrimp, cooked and peeled	8 lb (4 kg)
2 lb (1 kg)	mussels, cooked and shelled	8 lb (4 kg)
1 ½ qt (1 ½ L)	chicken broth or water	6 qt (6 L)
3 lb (1 ½ kg)	boneless chicken breasts and/or thighs	12 lb (5 kg)

In a small bowl, soak the saffron in just enough hot water to cover.

In a large frying pan, heat a layer of olive oil and sauté the onions, peppers, and garlic until softened. Do this in batches as necessary, adding more oil. Set aside.

In the same pan, brown the chorizo, followed by the calamari, which should be sautéed very briefly. Set both aside.

Sauté the rice in a few tablespoons of olive oil, 1 pound at a time until it is opaque, transferring each batch to a very large bowl or pot. Add the onion, pepper, and garlic mixture to the rice. Add the peas, parsley, the tomatoes coarsely chopped with their juice, the saffron with its soaking liquid, paprika, and oregano. Mix well and season generously with salt and pepper.

Add the chorizo, calamari, shrimp, and mussels to the rice mixture.

Cut the chicken in thick strips. Brown the chicken quickly in olive oil and distribute between 2 large roasting pans (use 8 for 100 servings). Cover the chicken with the rice mixture and add 2 to 3 cups of chicken broth or water to each pan. Cover tightly with 2 thicknesses of foil.

Bake in a moderate oven (325 F) for 1 hour or until the rice is thoroughly cooked. Check midway through, adding more chicken broth or water if rice becomes dry.

Wine suggestions: Rosé or a medium to full-bodied white, Muscat, Chardonnay.

Seafood Chowder

Many of the favorite meals served at Jim's are decidedly Franco-American. In this recipe, New England clam chowder meets bourride, a popular fish soup from Brittany. Fish replaces clams, which are hard to find in France. Frozen seafood works well for a big crowd, makes things easier for the cook, and definitely, saves you money. For richer chowder, you can replace the milk with cream.

For 25 servings		For 100 servings
½ lb (250 g)	salt pork or bacon, chopped	2 lb (1 kg)
4 oz (125 g)	butter	1 lb (500 g)
3	onions, chopped	4 lb (2 kg)
3 stalks	celery, chopped	12 stalks
5 lb (2 ½ kg)	boiling potatoes, peeled and diced	20 lb (8 kg)
2 qt (2 L)	fish broth, fresh or bouillon cubes	8 qt (8 L)
3	bay leaves	10
2 Tb	herbes de Provence	8 Tb
1 bunch	parsley, chopped	4 bunches
6 lb (2 ½ kg)	boneless white fish filets, cut in chunks	22 lb (10 kg)
1 lb (500 g)	scallops	4 lb (2 kg)
1 lb (500 g)	shrimp, peeled	4 lb (2 kg)
4 qt (4 L)	whole milk	16 qt (16 L)
	salt and pepper	

Lightly sauté the salt pork or bacon in butter a few minutes. Add the onions and celery and continue to sauté until the onion and celery are softened. Add the potatoes, the bay leaves, herbes de Provence, parsley, and enough fish broth to cover. Bring to a simmer and cook just until the potatoes are barely tender.

Add the fish, scallops, and shrimp along with the milk. Cook about 10 to 15 minutes. Do not overcook, as the shellfish will become tough. For the larger recipe, this step will take longer. Add salt and pepper to taste.

Wine suggestions: full-bodied white; Chardonnay, Gewürztraminer, Sémillon.

Salmon Leek Quiche

A savory tart makes a fine main course or appetizer any time of the year. It can be served warm or at room temperature. Often at Jim's dinners, two different tarts are served, one without meat. This provides variety and accommodates vegetarians. The following popular quiche uses ingredients that are easy to find and relatively inexpensive. A planning note: quiches may be baked ahead and reheated and, if wrapped very well, they may be frozen.

For 25 servings		For 100 servings
4	ready-made pie shells	16
8	large leeks	32
4 Tb	butter	½ lb (250 g)
4 lb (2 kg)	canned salmon, drained, flaked	16 lb (8 kg)
12	eggs	48
3 C (750 ml)	milk	3 qt (3 L)
1 tsp	salt	1 Tb
1 tsp	pepper	1 Tb
½ C	parsley, chopped	2 bunches
1 lb (500 g)	Gruyère, shredded	4 lb (2 kg)

If not pre-baked, pre-cook the pie shells (to avoid becoming soggy with the liquid filling). For an easy method, line the pie shells with foil, and prick them through the foil with a fork. Bake in a hot oven (425 F) for 10 minutes, remove foil, and cook 5 minutes more or until the pastry is just lightly colored.

Fill a large pan or sink with water and soak the leeks, letting the sand accumulate on the bottom. Lift out the leeks and drain. Remove the coarse outer leaves and cut the white and pale green parts into very thin rounds. You may also cut the leeks first and then soak them. Melt the butter in a large pan and cook the leeks slowly, covered, stirring occasionally until tender.

In a large bowl, beat the eggs lightly and add the milk, salt, and pepper. Gently, fold in the salmon, leeks, parsley and half of the cheese.

Baking 4 quiches at a time, ladle this mixture into 4 prepared pie shells. Sprinkle the reserved cheese over the tops. Bake the quiches in a hot oven (425 F) until they are slightly puffed, lightly browned, and the filling is set, about 40 minutes. For the large recipe, continue to bake the quiches in successive rounds.

Cool on racks and serve warm or cold cut into 8 pieces each.

Wine suggestions: full-bodied white; Chardonnay, Gewürztraminer.

Pâtes Au Thon (Tuna Pasta)

Catherine Monnet got this recipe from a Greek film director, who made up a batch one night for a big house-ful of children and adults from ingredients on his pantry shelf. Everyone adored it. It is an easy and economical dish and the sauce may be made a day ahead. A salad and a fruit dessert make good accompaniments.

For 25 servings		For 100 servings
4 oz (125 g)	butter	1 lb (500 g)
½ C (125 ml)	olive oil	2 C (500 ml)
2 lb (1 kg)	onions, chopped	8 lb (4 kg)
¼ C (1 head)	garlic, finely chopped	1 C (4 heads)
6 lb (3 kg)	canned tuna, drained	24 lb (12 kg)
1 bunch	parsley, chopped	4 bunches
1 ½ qt (1 ½ L)	crème fraîche (see recipe p.151)	6 qt (6 L)
	or heavy cream	
½ C (125 ml)	white wine	2 C (500 ml)
½ lb (250 g)	Parmesan cheese, grated	2 lbs (1 kg)
5 lb (2 ½ kg)	rigatoni or penne	18 lb (8 kg)
	olive oil	
	salt and pepper	
	herbes de Provence or dried thyme	

Melt the butter with the olive oil and sauté the onions and garlic until softened. Add the tuna, parsley, and cream. Heat to just under a boil and add the white wine. Stir in the Parmesan cheese. Set aside or if it is to be served at a later time, cool down, and refrigerate.

Cook 2 to 3 pounds of pasta at a time in plenty of boiling salted water. When barely tender or at the 'al dente' point, immediately drain the pasta into a colander. Plunge the colander into a sink of cold water or run cold water over until the pasta has cooled down. Drain well and put the cooked pasta into large roasting or baking pans. Add salt and pepper, a generous sprinkling of herbes de Provence or dried thyme and enough olive oil to lightly coat the pasta. Mix well.

When ready to serve, heat the pasta, lightly covered with foil in a 300 F degree oven for 10 to 15 minutes. Bring the sauce just to the boiling point. Serve the pasta in shallow bowls or plates with a ladle of sauce on top.

Wine suggestions: dry to medium-bodied white; Pinot Blanc, Riesling.

CHICKEN and TURKEY

Chicken Pasanda in Cashew Nut Sauce

Antonia Hoogewerf cooks terrific Indian meals in Jim's kitchen. Here's how she started: "I met Jim one May evening at the Café La Palette. Little did I know that I would soon be embroiled in a different world, one of a little atelier in a leafy alley in the 14th arrondissement where painters, writers, musicians, journalists, travelers, and people who just wander in come to have dinner with Jim and have been doing so for the last thirty-odd years. Shortly after we met, Jim found himself stranded without a cook and a hundred people coming to dinner. I had often catered for large parties at my home so I was not too daunted and offered to help. Jim was clearly scared I could not do it! I persuaded him to let me try an Indian dinner, which luckily worked out pretty well. This mild chicken dish from southern India has a wonderfully thick and nutty sauce and is best served with plain boiled rice."

For 25 servings		For 100 servings
6	onions, chopped	6 lb (2 ½ kg)
6 Tb	tomato purée	1 (29 oz or 765g) can
½ lb (250 g)	cashew nuts	2 lb (1 kg)
1 ½ Tb	garam masala	6 Tb
1 Tb	chili powder	4 Tb
3 Tb	lemon juice	12 Tb
1 ½ Tb	turmeric	6 Tb
1 Tb	salt	4 Tb
6 Tb	plain yogurt	1 ½ C (375 ml)
6 Tb	olive oil	1 ½ C (375 ml)
7 lb (3 kg)	boneless chicken, cubed	27 lb (12 kg)
3 bunches	cilantro, chopped	10 bunches
4 Tb	golden raisins	1 C (150 g)
1 lb (500 g)	mushrooms, quartered	4 lb (2 kg)
1 qt (1 L)	water or chicken broth	4 qt (4 L) water

Working in batches, combine the onions in a blender or food processor with the tomato purée, nuts, garam masala, chili powder, lemon juice, turmeric, salt, and yogurt and blend thoroughly. Transfer the mixture to a large bowl as you proceed with the blending. When all ingredients are blended, stir well.

In an extra large pot (or divided between two large pots), heat the olive oil and pour in the spice mixture. Cook gently over low heat. Add half of the chopped cilantro, the chicken, and raisins and continue to cook for just a few minutes. Add mushrooms, pour in water or broth to cover, and simmer, covered, for about 30 minutes or until chicken is cooked.

Serve hot with rice and garnish with the remaining chopped cilantro.

Wine suggestions: Many prefer beer with Indian food but if you serve wine, a dry white would be good, perhaps, a Riesling.

Moroccan Chicken with Lemon and Olives

This recipe traditionally uses whole chickens but for a large party, chicken thighs and breasts are more practical. In Paris, many shops carry preserved Moroccan lemons, which give this dish a particular tangy taste. If you have the time, they are easy to prepare or you may substitute fresh lemons. Also important is the ras el hanout, which means "top of the shop," a spice mixture than can include up to forty spices. This is available at specialty food stores (Vann's spice company makes it) or you can make a tasty blend with the recipe below.

For 25 servings		For 100 servings
10 lb (5 kg)	bone-in chicken (thighs and breasts)	40 lb (18 kg)
	salt and pepper	
3 bunches	parsley, chopped	10 bunches
4 Tb	garlic, chopped	½ C (2 heads)
4	onions, chopped	4 lb (2 kg)
2	cinnamon sticks	8
2 Tb	ras el hanout*	8 Tb
1 tsp	saffron (optional)	4 tsp
½ lb (250 g)	butter	2 lb (1 kg)
3	preserved or fresh lemons**	12
1 ½ C (6 lemons)	lemon juice	1 ½ qt (24 lemons)
4 oz (125 g)	green olives, pitted	1 lb (500 g)

Season the chicken generously with salt and pepper and place in a large pot. Add the parsley, reserving ¼ cup (1 cup for 100 servings), garlic, onions, cinnamon sticks, ras el hanout, saffron, and half the butter. If using fresh lemons, chop them and add now (you will use the entire lemon, rind included). Add water to cover and bring to a boil. Simmer covered for 30 to 40 minutes. The chicken should be *very* tender.

Remove chicken from broth using a strainer or slotted spoon and set aside. Remove the bones and shred the meat but not too finely. Remove and discard the cinnamon sticks from the broth.

Bring the broth to a boil and reduce by nearly half or until it is rich and thickened. If using preserved lemons, rinse them thoroughly and chop. Add remaining parsley, olives, preserved lemons, lemon juice, remaining butter, and the shredded chicken, cover and cook until just hot. Can be made a day in advance and reheated.

Serve this with couscous and pita bread.

Wine suggestions: medium to full-bodied white; Chardonnay or Muscat.

*Ras el Hanout

1 Tb ground mace
4 tsp each: nutmeg, ginger and salt
3 tsp allspice
2 tsp each: aniseed, cinnamon, black pepper, clove, turmeric
1 tsp each: cardamom, cayenne pepper

Combine all ingredients. Makes approximately 8 tablespoons.

**Preserved Lemons

In North African cuisine, preserved lemons play an important part in various stews and tajines. The entire lemon is eaten, usually cut in a small dice or strips, but must be rinsed first to remove excess salt. Preserved lemon is also delicious in risottos, vegetable salads and with fish. It is easy to prepare but allow time: it takes a week to 'cure'.

For 25 servings		For 100 servings
5	lemons, organic or untreated	20
½ C (150 g)	coarse salt	2 C (600 g)
	olive oil	
1	pint jar(s)	4

Wash and dry the lemons well. Cut 3 of the lemons (12 for 100 servings) into 8 wedges. In a large mixing bowl, combine the wedges with the salt. Push the lemons into the jars (it will be a tight fit), pressing to bring out the juice.

Juice a few of the remaining lemons adding enough juice to the jars just to cover and close with a non-metallic lid. Leave the jars out at room temperature shaking daily to combine the salt and juices. After 7 days, open the jars, add a little olive oil to cover and then, reseal and refrigerate.

Keeps 1 month.

Party Thighs

Yes, folks, these thighs are partiers: yummy, effortless, and easy on the wallet. Get them ready early in the day and bake them fairly close to serving time and brace yourself for the compliments.

For 25 servings		For 100 servings
9 lb (4 kg)	chicken thighs, boneless and skinless*	36 lb (16 kg)
12 oz (350 g)	butter, softened	3 lb (1½ kg)
2 Tb	Dijon mustard	8 Tb
2 Tb	red wine vinegar	8 Tb
1 Tb	paprika	4 Tb
1 Tb	salt	4 Tb
2 tsp	pepper	3 Tb
4 C (400 g)	breadcrumbs or saltine cracker crumbs	16 C (1½ kg)

Arrange the chicken on baking sheets and pat dry, if necessary.

In a bowl, cream the butter with the mustard, vinegar, and seasonings until smooth. Spread a small amount of the butter/mustard mixture over each thigh. Cover with a layer of crumbs.

Bake in a moderate (350 F) oven for about 40 minutes or until lightly browned.

*Boneless chicken is easier to eat standing up but bones add flavor. If your space and crowd permit, try this with bone-in thighs. You will need about 14 pounds for 25 servings (50 pounds for the large recipe).

Wine suggestions: medium to full-bodied white; Chardonnay or an oaky Sauvignon Blanc. Light red such as Gamay (Beaujolais) would also go well with this dish.

Chicken in Thai Green Curry

This Thai curry probably gets more positive comments and requests for seconds than nearly any other main dish. Slicing the chicken is the only time consuming part of this recipe. Made the morning or afternoon of your party, it can be reheated and served with basmati or jasmine rice. The green curry is nicely spicy but does not overwhelm the delicacy of the lime leaves, Thai basil, and coconut milk.

For 25 servings		For 100 servings
8 lb (4 kg)	chicken, boneless	32 lb (14 kg)
4 cans	coconut milk, canned	16 cans
7 oz (200 g)	green curry paste	28 oz (800 g)
8	lime leaves	32
1 C (250 ml)	fish sauce	1 qt (1 L)
2 Tb	sugar	8 Tb
2 C	peas, frozen	2 ½ lb (1 kg)
1 bunch	Thai basil	4 bunches

Slice chicken very thinly in strips.

Heat about 1/3 of the coconut milk on high heat until it boils. Add curry paste, lower heat to medium. Stir. Add half of the remaining coconut milk, raise heat and cook for about 8 minutes or until the oil of the milk rises to the top and the sauce thickens somewhat. Tear the lime leaves in thirds and add. Lower the heat and simmer for 2 minutes.

Add chicken, turn up heat, stir, and add last quantity of coconut milk. Add a few cups of water or enough just to cover the chicken. When bubbling, add the fish sauce and sugar, and cook, stirring, for 2 minutes.

Add the peas and basil, stir a minute and turn off the heat. At serving time, reheat gently.

Wine suggestions: dry to medium white; Sauvignon Blanc, Pinot Gris. Thai beer is also a good choice.

Sweet and Salty Chicken

Lucky Jim! His good friend, Barbara Sherman happens to be an excellent cook who often can be persuaded to cook for the Sunday night dinners. This is her recipe and is always a hit with the crowd. There are two stages to the preparation: the first part is done the day before and the second part just before baking. It is a very simple dish to prepare and people beg for seconds.

For 25 servings		For 100 serving
2 Tb	garlic, chopped finely	½ C (2 heads)
6 Tb	dried oregano	1 ½ C (180 g)
8 oz (500 ml)	red wine vinegar	2 qt (2 L)
9	bay leaves	3 dozen
2 C (500 ml)	olive oil	2 qt (2 L)
8 lb (4 kg)	boneless chicken, cubed	32 lb (14 kg)
4 oz (125 g)	capers and their juice	1 lb (500 g)
8 oz (250 g)	apricots or pitted prunes	2 lb (1 kg)
4 oz (125 g)	green olives, pitted	1 lb (500 g)
1 C (200 g)	brown sugar	4 C (800 g)
2 C (500 ml)	white wine	2 qt (2 L)

In a large (3-gallon) bowl, combine the garlic, oregano, vinegar, bay leaves, caper juice, olive oil, and vinegar. For the larger recipe, use 2 bowls.

Add the chicken, apricots or prunes, olives, capers, and stir. Cover with plastic wrap and let marinate for 24 hours in the refrigerator.

About 2 hours before serving, divide the chicken and the marinade between 2 (9 x 13-inch) baking pans or a large roasting pan. For 100 servings, use 8 (9 x 13-inch) baking pans or 4 large roasting pans. Sprinkle ½ cup brown sugar over each pan, followed by 1 cup of the white wine over each pan.

Bake in a moderately hot oven (350 F) for 1 hour. Serve with rice or parsley potatoes.

Wine suggestions: dry white; Pinot Blanc, Pinot Grigio. Ask your wine specialist about dry white Spanish and Italian wines.

Salade Olivier

Mary Bartlett first had this incredible chicken salad at a wake in California. No disrespect intended but the salad was so good, it had a rousing effect on everyone's spirits. This is a very smooth textured salad that has you wondering, is this an egg salad? A potato salad? A splendid treat whatever the occasion.

For 25 servings		For 100 servings
4 lb (2 kg)	chicken breast, boneless	16 lb (7 kg)
4 lb (2 kg)	baking potatoes, peeled	16 lb (7 kg)
1 lb (500 g)	frozen peas	4 lb (2 kg)
1	shallot(s), finely minced	4
5	hard boiled eggs, finely chopped	20
3 C (700 g)	mayonnaise	12 C (2 ½ kg)
½ C (125 ml)	sour cream or crème fraîche (see recipe p.151)	2 C (500 ml)
6 Tb	Dijon mustard	1½ C (250 g)
½ C (2 lemons)	lemon juice	2 C (10–12 lemons)
	salt and pepper	
2 tsp	dried dill	3 Tb
	Or	
5 or 6 sprigs	fresh dill, chopped	1 bunch
	Optional garnishes:	
	Lettuce leaves, paprika, parsley sprigs, and capers	

Poach the chicken breast in salted water or broth to cover until just done. Cool and drain. Using your fingers, shred the chicken very finely.

Boil the potatoes until tender. Drain and cool. Chop very finely. Place the peas in a colander and run water over them to thaw slightly. Drain and set aside.

In a separate bowl, mix the mayonnaise, sour cream, mustard, lemon juice, salt, pepper, and dill. Combine the shredded chicken, potatoes, peas, minced shallot, and hard-boiled eggs in a large pan or bowl. Fold in the mayonnaise mixture and chill.

At serving time, arrange the salad on a platter(s). Put lettuce around the edges and sprinkle with paprika or more traditionally, make 2 intersecting stripes of paprika. Garnish with parsley sprigs and a few spoonfuls of drained capers if desired.

Wine suggestions: dry white; Sauvignon Blanc, Chenin Blanc, Chardonnay; French Chablis or Vouvray.

Claudia's Prizewinning Chile Blanco

Claudia Bushee's chile won a prize in Reno, Nevada but its fame has spread to Paris where it has become a favorite at Jim's Sunday night dinners. Fast and easy, this chile can be cooked days in advance. Add a salad, some bread or rice and dinner is ready.

For 25 servings		For 100 servings
8 lb (4 kg)	boneless chicken, diced	30 lb (12 kg)
4 lb (2kg)	small white beans (cannelini), canned	15 1b (7 kg)
2 lb (1 kg)	onions, chopped	7 lb (3 kg)
½ C (125 ml)	cooking oil	2 C (500 ml)
1 C (4 heads)	garlic, chopped	4 C (16 heads)
2 (7 oz) cans	diced green chiles (mild)	10 (7 oz) cans
½ C (60 g)	ground cumin	2 C (240 g)
6 Tb	dried oregano	1 ½ C (180 g)
1 tsp or to taste	cayenne, approximately	1–2 Tb
2 C (500 ml)	chicken broth, approximately	6 C (1 ½ l)
	Garnishes:	
2 C (500 ml)	sour cream	2 qt (2 L)
2 bunches	green onions, thinly sliced	8 bunches
1 bunch	cilantro	4 bunches
2 lb (1 kg)	tomatoes, diced	8 lb (4 kg)
1 lb (500 g)	shredded jack or cheddar cheese	4 lb (2 kg)

Put the chicken in a large stockpot and cover with water or water mixed with chicken stock base or broth. Bring to a boil; reduce to a simmer and cook, stirring occasionally until the chicken is cooked through (about 15 minutes). Drain and save the broth.

Sauté onions in oil until golden and soft using additional oil if necessary. Put the onions in a large pot and add the beans, spices and chicken. Add enough broth to cover everything.

Simmer 30 minutes or longer. Taste and add more seasoning as necessary.

At serving time, set out the garnishes in bowls.

Drink suggestions: Beer, but a Rosé or Gamay will also work well.

Flat Green Enchilada Casserole

This layered turkey enchilada recipe can be spicy or mild depending on your preference. Fresh chiles will make a very spicy version. The tomatillo sauce and the ground turkey mixtures can be made a day ahead. Once the casserole is put together, it can wait a few hours in the refrigerator before baking.

For 25 servings		For 100 servings
6 lb (2 ½ kg)	tomatillos	24 lb (10 kg)
	Or	
6 lb (2 ½ kg)	canned tomatillos	24 lb (10 kg)
½ C (2 heads)	garlic, chopped	2 C (8 heads)
6 lb (2 ½ kg)	ground turkey	24 lb (10 kg)
	salt and pepper	
3 lb (1 ½ kg)	cheese, grated (Monterey Jack or Cheddar)	12 lb (5 kg)
1 lb (500 g)	cream cheese	4 lb (2 kg)
2 bunches	cilantro, chopped	8 bunches
1 lb (500 g)	onions, chopped	4 lb (2 kg)
1 Tb	oregano, Mexican preferably	3 Tb
1 Tb	basil	3 Tb
1 lb	green chiles, diced, canned	4 lb
	Or	
12	large fresh Serrano chiles, sliced	46
36	corn tortillas	144

If you are using fresh tomatillos, remove the thin husks and wash in cold water. Put in a large pot and cover with water. Bring to a simmer and cook just until softened. Set aside. In the bowl of a food processor, combine the garlic and cream cheese. Add the prepared or canned tomatillos and enough of the liquid to make a smooth sauce. Stir in the dried herbs, cilantro and the diced green chiles or the fresh chile.

In a frying pan, sauté the onions in oil and add the ground turkey. Sauté until the turkey is just cooked. Season with salt and pepper. Combine with the tomatillo sauce.

Soften the tortillas by wrapping them in a clean dishtowel and microwaving them briefly. Do this in batches. In a (13 x 18-inch) baking or roasting pan, spoon about 1 cup of sauce on the bottom followed by overlapping 12 tortillas. Add a layer of the turkey and tomatillo sauce and a layer of shredded cheese. Repeat with 2 more layers ending with shredded cheese. You will use 36 tortillas per pan. For the larger recipe, use 4 pans.

Bake at 400 F for about 20 minutes or until bubbling.

Drink suggestion: Beer or Rosé.

BEEF and LAMB

Bœuf Bourguignon

Some dishes are particularly suited for large parties and boeuf Bourguignon is one of these. This classic of French cooking, a savory beef stew with red wine, onions, bacon and mushrooms can be cooked a day in advance which actually improves the flavor. Chopping, peeling, and sautéeing take a lot of time so be sure to have help and allow a few hours for these tasks. In Paris, small peeled white onions are sold frozen. If you can find these, they are a good substitute for the fresh ones and save a lot of work. Frozen mushrooms, however, are not a good choice—too mushy! Serve with parsley potatoes or noodles, a salad, and of course, red wine.

For 25 servings		For 100 servings
1 lb (500 g)	slab bacon	4 lb (2 kg)
1 C (250 ml)	cooking oil, approximately	3 C (750 ml)
2 Tb	garlic, chopped	½ C (2 heads)
6	carrots, sliced	4 lb (2 kg)
5	onions, sliced	4 lb (2 kg)
2 C (250 g)	flour	8 C (1 kg)
8 lb (4 kg)	stewing beef, cubed	32 lb (14 kg)
2 qt (2 L)	beef broth	8 qt (8 L)
2 ½ bottles	red wine	10 bottles
3	bay leaves	10
3 Tb	tomato paste	10 Tb
2 Tb	herbes de Provence or thyme	8 Tb
½ lb (250 g)	butter, approximately	2 lb (1 kg)
2 lb (1 kg)	small white onions, fresh or frozen	8 lb (4 kg)
2 lb (1 kg)	mushrooms	8 lb (4 kg)
1 bunch	parsley, finely chopped	4 bunches
	salt and pepper	

Chop the bacon into small pieces. Sauté until nicely brown and place in one or divide between two large cooking pots.

Using 1 or 2 large skillets, heat about ¼ inch of oil and sauté the garlic, sliced carrots, and onions until completely softened. Wipe out the skillets.

Put about 1 cup of the flour into a medium-sized bowl and add enough of the cubed beef to fill the bowl about halfway. Toss the beef lightly to coat with flour. Heat about ¼ inch of oil in the skillet until the oil is nearly smoking. Add the floured beef and brown it.

Adding more flour and oil as needed, continue to coat and brown the beef in batches. Do not coat all the beef at once as it will get wet and sticky and won't brown properly. Add each batch to the pot(s) with the onions and bacon.

Pour enough of the broth and wine to cover the beef and vegetables. Bring to a boil, lower the heat and add the bay leaves, tomato paste, herbes de Provence or thyme, salt, and pepper to taste. Simmer until the beef is tender about 1 ½ to 2 hours.

While the beef is cooking, peel the onions (if using fresh) and melt a few tablespoons of butter in a large skillet. Sauté the onions until lightly browned and just barely tender. Set aside. Do this in batches adding more butter as needed.

Using the same pan, quickly brown the mushrooms in butter, a batch at a time. Add the mushrooms and onions to the beef about 30 minutes before the stew is finished. Add the parsley at the end and check the seasoning.

If the sauce is too thin, drain it from the cooking pot and reduce at high heat in another pot. This will create a more unctuous sauce but this step can be omitted without compromising the dish.

Wine suggestions: light to medium-bodied red; Pinot Noir or Gamay; French Burgundy, or Beaujolais.

Chili con Carne

Jim Haynes loves chili and Catherine Monnet's time-tested recipe is a favorite. Her advice is to cook it slowly, taste often and trust your judgment when it comes to final seasonings. The beans and meat are cooked separately which vegetarians appreciate. In Paris, chili is served with cornbread, which is still considered rather exotic but always gets an enthusiastic reception.

For 25 servings		For 100 servings
3 lb (1 ½ kg)	dried red beans	11 lb (5 kg)
2	bay leaves	8
3 tsp	herbes de Provence or dried thyme	3 Tb
1–2 Tbs	cumin	4–8 Tbs
3 Tb	Mexican chili powder	10 Tb
2 Tb	oregano, Mexican preferably	8 Tb
1 C (250 ml)	olive oil, approximately	1 qt (1 L)
6 lb (3 kg)	ground beef	22 lb (10 kg)
1 lb (500 g)	hot chorizo	4 lb (2 kg)
1 ½ lb (750 g)	onions, chopped	6 lb (3 kg)
2 Tb	garlic, finely chopped	½ C (2 heads)
3	green peppers, chopped	12
3 cans	tomatoes, canned (29 oz/765 g)	10 cans

1 bunch	parsley, chopped	4 bunches
1 C (250 ml)	beef broth (fresh or bouillon cubes)	1 qt (1 L)
	salt and pepper	
	Tabasco to taste	
10 oz (300 g)	shredded mild cheese	3 lb (1¼ kg)

Sort through the beans and throw out bad ones. Wash the beans and soak overnight in a volume of water that is about 4 times the quantity of beans.

Drain the beans and place in a very large cooking pot with the bay leaves, and herbes de Provence. Add enough water to cover the beans by about 2 inches. Cover the pot and simmer until tender, adding more water if necessary. This may take a few hours. Season with salt to taste, half the cumin, chili powder, and oregano. Continue to simmer about 20 minutes.

While the beans are cooking, brown the meat in a few tablespoons of olive oil using one or two large skillets. You will have to do this in several batches, adding more oil as needed. Place each batch of browned meat into a very large pot.

Wipe out the skillet(s); heat a few tablespoons of olive oil, and lightly sauté the onion, garlic, and green pepper. Sauté this mixture in batches as necessary and add to the meat.

Roughly, chop the tomatoes and stir them into the meat with the remaining cumin, chili powder, oregano. Add the parsley. Simmer for 1 to 2 hours.

Taste the chile and the beans for seasoning, adding extra salt, spices, and Tabasco as desired. Serve a ladle of both the meat and beans in bowls with grated cheese. Have additional hot sauce available on the side. Rice and cornbread are good accompaniments.

Drink suggestions: Beer; but a full-bodied red, such as Zinfandel or Tempranillo, would also be good.

Moussaka

In Greece, Turkey, and other countries, moussaka comes in many different versions. For many of us, however, moussaka suggests eggplant. This recipe takes time to prepare but it is a one-dish meal that needs no accompaniment other than sliced baguette or rice. You can roast or grill all the eggplant a day in advance. The meat mixture and the béchamel sauce can also be prepared in advance, leaving only the assembly to do on the day it is baked.

For 25 servings		For 100 servings
6 lb (2 ½ kg)	eggplants	22 lb (10 kg)
1 C (250 ml)	olive oil, approximately	1 qt (1 L)
1 lb (500 g)	onions, chopped	4 lb (2 kg)
2 Tb	garlic, finely chopped	½ C (2 heads)
6 lb (2 ½ kg)	ground beef or lamb	22 lb (10 kg)
1 can	tomatoes, canned (29 oz or 765g)	3 cans
½ bottle	red wine	2 bottles
½ bunch	parsley, chopped	2 bunches
2 Tb	dried oregano	8 Tb
2 tsp	cinnamon	2 Tb
1 tsp	nutmeg	1 ½ Tb
	salt and pepper	

Sauce Béchamel (White Sauce)

8 oz (250 g)	butter	2 lb (1 kg)
1 C (125 g)	flour	4 C (500 g)
2 qt (2 L)	milk	8 qt (8 L)
nutmeg		
salt, pepper		

Slice the eggplants into ½ inch round slices and sprinkle with salt. Let the eggplant rest about 1 hour to draw out liquid. Pat dry, brush each slice with olive oil and arrange overlapping on baking sheets. Bake about 20 minutes or until soft. Set aside. This step may be done in advance.

If you prefer to grill eggplant, brush both sides with olive oil or cooking oil and cook on a hot grill about 2 minutes per side.

Using 1 or 2 large skillets, heat about ¼ inch of oil and sauté the onions and garlic until softened and set aside. Do this in batches, as necessary.

Using the same pan, add additional oil and sauté the beef or lamb until lightly browned. As each batch browns, place it in a very large pot.

Add the cooked onion and garlic mixture, tomatoes, red wine, parsley, oregano, cinnamon, and nutmeg to the browned meat. Simmer slowly about 30 minutes. Season with salt and pepper.

While the meat mixture simmers, prepare the béchamel sauce. Melt the butter in a large pot until it is bubbling. Whisk in the flour gradually and continue to stir for about 8 to 10 minutes over low heat without browning the mixture. Heat the milk in a large pan or in the microwave. Gradually, add the hot milk to the flour mixture stirring continuously. Add nutmeg, salt, and pepper to taste. Bring to a boil, lower the heat, and whisk a few minutes until thickened. Taste and correct the seasoning. For 100 servings, this sauce will take quite a lot of time and stirring. Making it in 2 batches is a practical alternative.

Oil 2 (9 x 13-inch) baking pans or 1 large roasting pan. Using half of the eggplant slices, distribute them on the bottom of each pan. For 100 servings, use 8 (9 x 13-inch) pans or 4 large roasting pans. Top with meat mixture followed by the remaining eggplant.

Spread the sauce evenly over the eggplant. Bake in a moderate oven (325 F) for about 1 hour. The béchamel should be lightly browned. Let the moussaka sit about 10 minutes before cutting into squares. It may be served at room temperature.

Wine suggestions: Rosé or medium-bodied white; Muscat, Viognier. Many good inexpensive whites are available from Greece.

Sabz Ghost (Lamb in Coconut Milk)

Antonia Hoogewerf's Indian dinners are among the most popular at Jim's Sunday night soirées. "Indian cooking is not a precise art, although a fine and subtle one. The trick with spices is to keep tasting and trying it out on those around you. Be careful with chilies, as not everyone likes a very spicy dish. I use small, hot, green chilies and yogurt, cream, or coconut milk to cool things down. Remember fresh chilies continue to get hotter the longer they cook." Sabz ghost, a famous and deceptively simple Indian dish, is exotically spiced yet mild and creamy.

For 25 servings		For 100 servings
8 lb (4 kg)	lamb, cubed	32 lb (14 kg)
½ C (2 heads)	garlic, finely minced	2 C (8 heads)
1 (5-inch) piece	ginger, peeled and finely chopped	4 (5-inch) pieces
½ C (125 ml)	cooking oil	2 C (500 ml)
8 oz (250 g)	whole blanched almonds	2 lb (1 kg)
1 C (150 g)	raisins	1 lb (500 g)
6	cardamom pods	24
6	whole cloves	24
	salt and pepper	

1 C (250 ml)	plain yogurt	1 qt (1 L)
1	green chili pepper	5
1	dried red pepper	5
2 cans	coconut milk, 5.6 oz, unsweetened (more may be needed)	8 cans
1 bunch	cilantro, chopped	4 bunches

Marinate the lamb in a large bowl with the garlic and ginger for 2 hours. In a very large pot or divided between two pots, heat the oil and fry the almonds and raisins for just a few minutes or until they are lightly browned. Set aside. Using the same oil, add the cardamom, cloves, and the lamb and brown, stirring, over high heat

Mix in salt, pepper, and yogurt. Lower the heat and cook until the yogurt is completely absorbed (about 30 minutes). Stir in the red and green chili peppers and half of the chopped cilantro. Add coconut milk and cook on a low flame, stirring regularly, for about 40 minutes to an hour. When the lamb is tender, add the almonds and raisins. Cover the pan and simmer until the sauce is reduced.

Taste for seasoning, adding additional coconut milk if too spicy. Garnish with the remaining chopped cilantro and serve hot, with chutney, Naan bread, and rice.

Wine suggestions: dry to medium-bodied white; Pinot Blanc, Riesling, Chardonnay. As with many Indian dishes, beer is popular.

Keftedes (Mid-Eastern meatballs)

Jim's atelier, with its large glass windows, gives onto a lovely garden. In the summer, the doors are opened and the party spills out into the garden. This is the time of year the guest list hits numbers well over one hundred. Many travelers to Paris want the experience of joyfully eating outdoors when it stays light until ten or eleven at night. For a splendid late night outdoor feast of your own, serve these meatballs with taboulé, hummus, and a green salad.

For 25 servings		For 100 servings
1 lb (500 g)	onions, finely chopped	2 lb (2 kg)
2 Tb	garlic, finely chopped	½ C (2 heads)
½ C (125 ml)	olive oil, approximately	2 C (500 ml)
8 lb (4 kg)	ground beef or lamb or a mixture	32 lb (14 kg)
6	eggs, beaten lightly	24
2 C (200 g)	dried bread crumbs, approximately	8 C (800 g)
1 C (250 ml)	tomato sauce	1 qt (1 L)
1 C (150 g)	dried currants	20 oz (600 g)
2 Tb	dried mint, crumbled	8 Tb
2 tsp	cinnamon	4 Tb
	salt and pepper	
1 lb (500 g)	sesame seeds	4 lb (2 kg)
2 C (500 ml)	cooking oil, approximately	2 qt (2 L)

Using 1 or 2 large skillets, heat a few tablespoons of olive oil and sauté the finely chopped onion and garlic until soft. Continue to add oil and sauté this mixture in batches as necessary. Cool.

In a large bowl, combine the onion garlic mixture and the ground meat. Add the eggs, tomato sauce, dried currants, mint, cinnamon, salt, and pepper to taste. Add enough breadcrumbs so that the mixture holds together. Form the meat into balls, or short cigar shapes and roll into sesame seeds. Brown lightly, in oil.

Place in baking trays and finish cooking about 20 minutes in a moderate oven (350F). Keep warm, covered with foil to avoid drying out.

Wine suggestions: dry to medium red; Pinot Noir, Gamay, Syrah. There are also some good and inexpensive Greek and Middle-Eastern reds.

Navarin of Lamb

"I live in Montparnasse close to Jim's atelier. In April, it's still a little chilly but my neighborhood market has plenty of young lamb and spring vegetables, which makes me think of this special stew" Mary Bartlett has found that these baby turnips, carrots, and potatoes have very thin skins so that peeling is not necessary. What a timesaver! This stew can be made in advance and reheated.

For 25 servings		For 100 servings
8 lb (4 kg)	lamb, cubed	25 lb (11 kg)
4 oz (125 g)	butter, approximately	1 lb (500 g)
½ C (70 g)	flour	2 C (250 g)
6 Tb	tomato paste	1 can (29 oz/765 g)
1 bottle	white wine	4 bottles
2 Tb	garlic, chopped	½ C (2 heads)
	Bouquets garnie:	
4 sprigs	thyme	1 bunch
4	bay leaves	10
8 sprigs	parsley	1 bunch
4 lb (2 kg)	small potatoes	18 lb (8 kg)
2 lb (1 kg)	carrots, sliced	9 lb (4 kg)
2 lb (1 kg)	baby onions or shallots, peeled	9 lb (4 kg)
2 lb (1 kg)	small turnips	9 lb (4 kg)
1 ½ lb	frozen baby peas	6 lb (3 kg)
½ C	parsley, chopped	2 bunches
1 Tb	salt	4 Tb
2 tsp	pepper	3 Tb

If necessary, trim any excess fat from the lamb. Melt a few tablespoons of butter in 1 or 2 large skillets until hot and bubbling and, working in batches, sauté the lamb until lightly browned, setting aside each batch. When sautéed, put the lamb in a very large pot or divide it between two large pots, sprinkle with the flour and stir to coat well.

If you are using two pots, divide the ingredients for the bouquet garnie into 2 piles and tie each tightly with string. Add equal portions of the tomato paste to the lamb and stir well. Add the wine, enough water to cover the meat, the bouquets garnies, salt, and pepper. Bring to a boil, lower to simmer, and cook for 30 minutes.

Add the potatoes and carrots, dividing them between two pots as necessary. If the level of liquid is not sufficient, add more wine and water in equal parts. Raise the heat until the navarin approaches a boil and then simmer 15 minutes.

Add the onions and turnips and continue to simmer 30 minutes. Add the peas for a final 5 minutes. Remove the bouquets and taste for salt and pepper. Add parsley and stir well.

Wine suggestions: either lighter reds (Pinot Noir or Gamay) or a medium-bodied white (Chardonnay). Traditionally served in France with Beaujolais or red Burgundy, or a white Mâcon.

PORK and VEAL

Cassoulet (White Bean Stew)

In the many versions of this traditional southwestern French recipe, white beans are the only agreed upon element. After that, it gets complicated. Lamb, pork, sausages from Toulouse, and delicious but pricy confit de canard (preserved duck legs) are some of the options. This variation calls for pork, sausages, and pigs' feet, and a crunchy breadcrumb topping. Omit the feet if you wish, but they add great flavor to the beans.

For 25 servings		For 100 servings
4 lb (2 kg)	small white beans	16 lb (8 kg)
4	onions, chopped	4 lb (2 kg)
4	carrots, chopped	3 lb (1 ½ kg)
¼ C (1 head)	garlic, chopped	1 C (4 heads)
1 Tb	herbes de Provence	4 Tb
1 lb (500 g)	slab bacon, cubed	4 lb (2 kg)
1-2	pig's feet, quartered, (optional)	5
3 ½ lb (1 ½ kg)	pork, cubed	14 lb (6 kg)
	salt and pepper	
3 ½ lb (1 ½ kg)	sausages, sweet Italian	14 lb (6 kg)
4 C (250 g)	bread crumbs	2 lb (1 kg)

A planning note: if you wish, the beans may be prepared a few days in advance.

Sort through the beans and throw out bad ones. Wash the beans and soak for 6 hours or overnight in a volume of water that is about 4 times the quantity of beans. Drain and cook with onion, carrot, garlic, herbes de Provence, bacon, pigs' feet, and enough water to cover for 1 ½ hours. Add the pork and cook 1 hour longer. Stir often to avoid scorching. When the beans are tender, season with salt and pepper to taste. Scoop off some of the liquid from the beans.

Remove pig's feet and let cool. Separate the meat from the bones and chop it finely. Add this meat back into the beans. Discard the bones. Now, if preparing in advance, the bean mixture may be cooled down and refrigerated for one or two days.

Brown the sausages quickly in a large frying pan in batches. Cut in 1-inch serving pieces. Distribute the sausages between two roasting pans and cover with beans. Sprinkle the breadcrumbs on top and cook in a moderately hot oven (350 F) for 1 hour.

For the larger recipe (using 6 to 8 pans), prepare only as many pans as your oven will accommodate at one time and bake in two rounds.

Reheat, uncovered, at serving time.

Wine suggestions: full-bodied red; Merlot, Cabernet Sauvignon, Malbec, or French Cahors, Madiran or Bordeaux.

Choux farcis au Riesling (Cabbage Rolls with Chestnuts and Riesling)

These cabbage rolls are a delicate and refined take on a homey dish. With Riesling and chestnuts, this recipe has Alsatian roots. If chestnuts are not easy for you to find, you may omit them and the rolls will still be delicious. There is a lot of fine chopping to do but filling the cabbage rolls is a pleasant task with the company of helpers. Madame Paupèrt, Jim's upstairs neighbor, helped make these one November afternoon. Although she does not attend the Sunday evening soirées, she approves of them and of her unusual neighbor, Jim. As part of the evening's tradition, one of Jim's guests always takes dinner upstairs to Madame Paupèrt.

For 25 servings (about 50 cabbage rolls)		For 100 servings (about 200 cabbage rolls)
3	green cabbages (Savoy)	10
½ lb (250 g)	butter	2 lb (1 kg)
4 Tb	cooking oil	1 C (250 ml)
2 lb (800 g)	carrots, finely diced	7 lb (3 kg)
2 lb (800 g)	onions, finely diced	7 lb (3 kg)
2 lb (800 g)	leeks, well washed, white and pale green parts only, finely diced	7 lb (3 kg)
2 lb (800 g)	tomatoes, finely diced	7 lb (3 kg)
2 lb (800 g)	chestnuts, diced (optional)	7 lb (3 kg)
2 tsp	thyme	2 Tb
1 bunch	parsley, chopped	4 bunches
1 tsp	nutmeg	1 Tb nutmeg
	salt and pepper.	
4 lb (2 kg)	ground veal, pork or a mixture	18 lb (8 kg)
2 bottles	Riesling	6 bottles

Prepare the leaves as follows:

Bring a large pot of salted water to a boil. With a small sharp knife, core the cabbages and carefully, break off the leaves. Discard the tough outer leaves. There should be approximately 15 to 20 large sized leaves per cabbage. Fill a large bowl or the sink with cold water. Taking a few leaves at a time, boil the cabbage about 5 minutes or until it is just tender. Refresh the leaves in cold water and stack on a rack or on towels. Cut out the tough inner membrane in a V-shape using a small knife or scissors.

Prepare the filling:

Heat the butter and oil in a large pot or divide it between two large pots. Sauté the carrots, onions, and leeks slowly until they are very soft but not browned. Add the tomatoes, chestnuts, and parsley and continue to sauté several more minutes. Add the thyme, nutmeg, salt, and pepper. Stir well and let cool.

When cool, add the vegetable mixture to the ground meat, folding and stirring to combine. Add additional salt and pepper and test the seasoning by cooking a tablespoon of the filling in a small skillet with a little oil. Taste and correct the seasoning.

Stuff each cabbage leaf with a small ball of filling, wrapping the leaf around it. Arrange the stuffed leaves, seam side down and close together in 2 roasting pans (use 8 for 100 servings). Pour the Riesling over the cabbage rolls and lay a sheet of parchment paper over each pan. Cover tightly with aluminum foil. Bake in a moderately hot oven (375 F) for about 45 minutes or until the interior of the cabbage rolls is cooked through.

For the larger recipe, prepare as many pans as your oven will accommodate. Refrigerate the remaining pans. Bake in two rounds. Keep covered and reheat at serving time.

Serve with rice or parsley potatoes.

Wine suggestions: dry to medium-bodied white; Riesling, Gewürztraminer.

Dillkött (Swedish Dill Veal Stew)

Ewa Rudling is a well-known photographer whose work is collected internationally. A dear friend of Jim's, Ewa cooked the following recipe on a Sunday night. Based on her grandmother's traditional Swedish recipe, she adapted it to accommodate the crowd. Making dillkött in advance is recommended. Like many stews, its flavor improves with a day's rest. You may use either veal or lamb in this recipe. The egg yolk enrichment, which creates a rich and silky sauce, is optional and this step should not be completed until close to serving time. Serve with parsley potatoes or rice.

For 25 servings		For 100 servings
8 lb (4 kg)	veal or lamb, cubed	32 lb (14 kg)
3	onions, halved	2 ¼ lb (1 kg)
2	carrots, halved	1 lb (500 g)
5	white pepper corns	1 Tb
2	whole cloves	1 tsp
4 lb (2 kg)	carrots, cut into rounds	18 lb (8 kg)
2 lb (1 kg)	leeks, white parts, in 1-inch pieces	9 lb (4 kg)

Sauce

4 oz (125 g)	butter	1 lb (500 g)
1 C (125 g)	flour	4 C (500 g)
3 qt (3 L)	cooking broth	10 qt (10 L)
2 C (500 ml)	crème fraîche (see recipe p.151) or heavy cream	2 qt (2 L)
6	egg yolks (optional)	24
1 bunch	dill, finely chopped	4 bunches
4 Tb	lemon juice or vinegar	1 C (250 ml)
1 Tb	sugar	4 Tb

Put the meat in a stockpot. Add cold water, 1 quart at a time, measuring as it is added, until the meat is covered. Add 1 teaspoon salt per quart added. Bring to a boil and remove any scum that collects on the surface. Lower the heat and add the onions, the halved carrots, peppercorns, and cloves.

Cook over low heat until the meat is tender, approximately 1 ½ hours. Remove the meat and set aside, lightly covered.

Strain the broth, discarding the onions, carrots, peppercorns, and cloves. Return the broth to the pot; add the sliced leeks and carrot rounds, simmering about 30 minutes until tender. Remove the vegetables and set aside, lightly covered.

Prepare a roux by melting the butter in a large saucepan and stirring in the flour. Cook for several minutes slowly, stirring. The roux should not brown. Add the hot broth a little at a time while stirring. Add enough to make a lightly thickened sauce. Boil the sauce for several minutes.

Add the cream to the sauce. (For the optional step, reserve half of the cream). Flavor with dill, lemon juice (or vinegar), and a few spoonfuls of sugar to make it sweet and sour. Combine the sauce with the meat and vegetables and reheat before serving.

For the optional enrichment with egg yolks, mix the reserved cream with the egg yolks in a large bowl. Draw off a few ladles of the hot sauce from the stew and add to the egg mixture, stirring well. Pour this mixture into the stew and stir thoroughly. Heat until quite hot but do not boil. Taste and adjust the seasoning.

Wine suggestions: medium to full-bodied white; Sauvignon Blanc, Sémillon.

Green Lentils and Sausages "A La Bonne Franquette"

This dinner is truly 'à la bonne franquette', which is to say simple and unfussy. The vegetarians who come to Jim's are pleased to discover that the lentils are cooked separately from the meat. Le Puy lentils are from the Auvergne area in France. Similar green lentils are found easily in the United States and are fine to use in this recipe. Green lentils take a very short time to cook. Be very careful not overcook them as much of their flavor is derived from a slight crunchiness. Both the sausages and lentils may be cooked in advance.

The Sausages:

For 25 servings		For 100 servings
7 lb (3 kg)	sausages, sweet Italian, cut in half	22 lb (10 kg)
2 Tb	cooking oil, approximately	½ C (125 ml)
6	red peppers, sliced	11 lb (5 kg)
8	onions, sliced	11 lb (5 kg)
¼ C (1 head)	garlic, chopped	1 C (4 heads)
2 Tb	thyme	8 Tb
2 Tb	olive oil	1 C (250 ml)
	salt and pepper	

In 1 or 2 large skillets, heat a few tablespoons of cooking oil over a high flame. Add enough sausages to fill the pan without overcrowding. Brown quickly on all sides and remove to a side dish. Continue with the remaining sausages, adding oil as necessary until all are browned.   Combine the peppers, onions, chopped garlic, thyme, salt, and pepper in a large bowl. Add enough olive oil to coat the mixture lightly. Mix thoroughly and divide between 1 or 2 large roasting pans (use 4 to 6 pans for 100 servings). This will be a bed for the sausages.

Divide the sausages between the baking pans arranging them in 1 layer and cover with foil. Bake in a moderately hot oven (350 F) for 40 minutes.

For the larger recipe, bake as above in as many pans as your oven will accommodate and refrigerate the rest. Bake in two or more rounds.

The sausages may be prepared a day ahead and reheated before serving.

The Lentils:

For 25 servings		For 100 servings
3 lb (1 ½ kg)	carrots, finely diced	11 lb (5 kg)
5 lb (2 ½ kg)	green lentils	18 lb (8 kg)
½ lb (250 g)	unsalted butter	2 lb (1 kg)
2 Tb	fresh thyme leaves	8 Tb
	salt and pepper	
1 jar each	Optional: hot mustard and sour pickles	4 jars each

Bring a large pot of water to a rolling boil and cook the carrots for approximately 10 minutes or until just tender. Drain and refresh with cold water. Set carrots aside.

In a large colander or sieve, rinse the lentils until running water. Place in a large pot or divide between two large pots. Add water to cover by 2 inches and bring to a boil, stirring occasionally. Lower the heat to a simmer and continue to cook until the lentils are just soft with some crunchiness. Check after 10 minutes. The lentils will be difficult to stir due to their volume but try not to over cook them. Drain off the water and put the lentils back into the pot or into a very large bowl to make the stirring easier. Add the diced carrots, the butter, thyme, salt and pepper. Mix and correct the seasoning.

The best way to reheat the lentils is to create a bain-marie or double boiler by putting the pot into a larger pot, partly filled with water. Keeping the lentils from the direct heat will avoid scorching.

To serve, top a portion of lentils with one or two sausages and a spoonful of the onions and peppers. Hot mustard and sour pickles make good self-serve accompaniments.

Wine suggestions: medium to full-bodied red; Cabernet Sauvignon, Merlot, Syrah/Grenache. Côtes du Rhône or red wines of the Languedoc.

Mainly Osso Buco (Braised Veal Stew)

Osso buco is a celebrated Italian dish with veal shanks and aromatic vegetables. These bones add a marvelous flavor and in Italy, there are even special spoons for extracting and eating the marrow. For a large party, however, it is difficult to prepare such a vast quantity of veal shanks. For this reason, the following veal stew recipe is 'mainly' osso buco: there is boneless veal in addition to the shanks and the meat is cut off the bones before cooking. The final touch? Gremolada. Considered indispensable by many Italian cooks, this fresh mixture of garlic, parsley, and lemon rind is sprinkled on top of the osso buco just before serving.

For 25 servings		For 100 servings
10 oz (300 g)	butter	2 ½ lb (1 kg)
5	carrots, chopped	4 lb (1 ¾ kg)
8	onions, chopped	8 lb (4 kg)
4 stalks	celery, chopped	3 lb (1 ½ kg)
¼ C (1 head)	garlic, chopped	1 C (4 heads)
7 lb (3 kg)	veal shanks	22 lb (10 kg)
3 lb (1 ½ kg)	boneless veal, cubed	12 lb (5 kg)
2 C (250 g)	flour	8 C (1 kg)
1 C (250 ml)	cooking oil, approximately	1 qt (1 L)
2 cans	tomatoes, canned (29 oz or 765 g)	5 cans
1 ½ qt (1 ½ L)	broth (chicken, beef or veal)	6 qt (6 L)
2 Tb	thyme	8 Tb
	salt and pepper	

2 lb (1 kg)	mushrooms, thickly sliced or quartered	8 lb (4 kg)
3 lemons	grated rind	12 lemons
1 bunch	parsley, chopped	4 bunches

Set aside 2 tablespoons of the chopped garlic (½ cup for 100 servings) for the gremolada.

Melt the butter until bubbling in a very large pot or divided between two pots. Add the onions, carrots, and celery and cook slowly over medium heat until the vegetables are completely softened. Add the remaining garlic, stir, and turn off the heat.

Cut the meat off the shank bones, and cut into 1-inch pieces. Reserve the bones. Put about 1 cup of the flour in a medium-sized bowl and add enough of the veal to fill the bowl about halfway. Toss lightly to coat with flour.

Heat about ¼ inch of oil in 1 or 2 large skillets until the oil is nearly smoking. Add a layer of floured veal and brown it.

Adding more flour as needed, continue to coat and brown the veal in batches. Do not coat all the veal at once as it will get wet and sticky and won't brown properly. As each batch browns, add it to the pot(s) of cooked vegetables.

Add the reserved shank bones, tomatoes, coarsely chopped and their juices, white wine, thyme, and just enough broth to cover the meat. Bring to boil, then lower the heat and cook about 2 hours or until very tender. Taste and adjust the seasoning. The stew can be cooled down, refrigerated, and reheated the following day.

As the stew is cooking, prepare the gremolata by combining the chopped parsley, the reserved garlic, and the grated lemon rind in a bowl.

To serve, reheat the osso buco and remove the bones. Stir in the gremolada. Osso buco can be served with rice or pasta or simply, as is, followed by a green salad.

Wine suggestions: medium-bodied red; Sangiovese, Nebbiolo; Italian Chianti or Montalcino.

Roast Pork

With a potato gratin or applesauce and some green vegetables, this roast makes a hearty winter meal. Or for a terrific hot weather meal, serve this versatile roast sliced at room temperature with black beans, rice, a salad, and hot sauce. Whatever the season, this pork roast can be cooked a day in advance. Allow a day or so for marinating as this makes the pork especially tender and flavorful.

For 25 servings		For 100 servings
9 lb (4 kg)	boneless pork loin	36 lb (16 kg)
4 Tb (1 head)	garlic, chopped	1 C (4 heads)
8 sprigs	thyme	1 bunch
1 Tb	coarse salt	8 Tb
2 tsp	pepper	4 Tb
1 C (250 ml)	cooking oil, approximately	1 qt (1 L)
4	carrots, chopped	3 lb (1 ½ kg)
5	onions, sliced	5 lb (2 ½ kg)

Tie the pork loins securely with string, cutting if necessary to fit into the roasting pans.

Prepare the dry marinade: mix the garlic, thyme, salt, and pepper together, and rub into all sides of the pork loins. Place the meat in plastic bags, set in pans, and refrigerate up to 48 hours, turning occasionally.

Distribute the sliced onions and carrots between 2 (11 x 14-inch) roasting pans (use 5 pans for 100 servings). Thoroughly scrape off the marinade. This is an important step to avoid over-saltiness. Dry the meat with paper towels, then sauté on all sides in a hot skillet in a few tablespoons of oil until browned. After browning, place the pork loins in the prepared roasting pans, fitting 2 or 3 to each pan. Cover tightly with aluminum foil.

Roast covered in a moderately hot oven (350 F) for about 2 hours. The pork will be very tender and have given off quite a lot of juice. Serve sliced with the juices and vegetables either hot or at room temperature.

Wine suggestions: drier reds (Pinot Noir, Sangiovese) or full-bodied whites (Chardonnay, Sémillon).

New Orleans Red Beans and Rice

Jodi Poretto, a longtime friend of Jim's from New Orleans, strapped on an apron over her chic little black dress and declared she was ready to cook. "I arrived in Paris in 1985 to attend graduate school and that's when I heard about the Sunday night dinners. I first prepared red beans and rice one weekend when Jim needed a cook. Being from Louisiana, where life is a party, I think it is lots of fun to prepare dinner for one hundred people."

For 25 servings		For 100 servings
3 lb (1 ½ kg)	dried red beans	11 lb (5 kg)
2 lb (1 kg)	onion, chopped	7 lb (3 kg)
1	green pepper(s), chopped	4
2 stalks	celery, chopped	8 stalks
½ lb (250 g)	thick bacon, diced	2 lb (1 kg)
½ lb (250 g)	ham, cubed	2 lb (1 kg)
2 lb (1 kg)	chorizo, moderately spicy	9 lb (4 kg)
2 Tb	garlic, chopped	½ C (2 heads)
4 Tb	oregano	1 C (120 g)
8 Tb	parsley, chopped	2 bunches
2	bay leaves	7
	salt	
	cayenne and black pepper	
1 C (250 ml)	red wine	1 bottle

Sort through the beans and throw out bad ones. Wash the beans and soak overnight in a volume of water that is about 4 times the quantity of beans.

Drain the beans, place in a large pot, and add water to cover by 2 inches. Add the seasonings and the meat but not the red wine. Bring to a boil, and simmer for 3 hours.

Add red wine and simmer until the beans are tender and creamy, about 30 minutes to an hour. Serve with long grain rice.

Wine suggestions: Rosé to lighter reds, Gamay.

VEGETARIAN

Eggplant with Almonds

From Mary Bartlett: "I first ate this dish at a friend's house in the south of France. This method of cooking eggplant is ridiculously simple and can be done on the morning of your party. The eggplants will look squashed and wrinkled but taste marvelous." For a main course, count on a whole eggplant per serving. You can halve the recipe and serve this as an appetizer.

For 25 servings		For 100 servings
25	medium eggplants	100
	salt and pepper	
3 cloves	garlic, chopped finely	12 cloves
	Lemon Vinaigrette (see recipe p.54)	
½ lb (250 g)	almonds, slivered	2 lb (1 kg)

Wash the eggplants and line them up on baking sheets. Prick each one all over with a fork. Bake in a hot over (400 F) until tender; about 40 minutes.

Let cool. Prepare the vinaigrette.

At serving time, split each eggplant in 2 lengthwise and season with salt and pepper. Add the garlic to the lemon vinaigrette and spoon some over each half. Toast the almonds in either a dry pan or the microwave, taking care not to burn them. Sprinkle about 1 tablespoon of almonds over each serving.

Serve the eggplant with cornbread, pita bread, or garlic toasts and a hearty salad such as Caesar (p.43) or the green salad with fennel, sun-dried tomatoes, and pine nuts (p.48).

Wine suggestions: dry to medium-bodied white; Sauvignon Blanc, Riesling, Pinot Blanc

Vegetable Pad Thai

What makes pad Thai an excellent choice for a crowd is the fact that the noodles do not need to be cooked. This saves time and effort and, as a bonus, this dish can be made in advance and tastes fantastic. As to the ingredients, these are easily found in stores carrying Asian products. 'Sauce for chicken' are the exact words that will appear on the bottle's label. It is a sweet red chili sauce. Tamarind pulp is sold in cellophane-covered blocks and contains seeds. It's a little messy to work with but has a particular sour taste that is important for an authentic pad Thai.

½ package	tamarind pulp	2 packages
2 Tb	sugar	½ C (100 g)
¾ C (187 ml)	fish sauce*	3 C (750 ml)
10	limes	40
4 Tb	'sauce for chicken'	1 C (250 ml)
3 lb (1 kg)	assorted vegetables, fresh or frozen (broccoli, carrots, peapods, sliced thinly)	9 lb (4 kg)
2 Tb	garlic, minced	½ C (2 heads)
2 Tb	garlic chili paste	8 Tb
2 bunches	sliced scallions	5 bunches
3 lb (1 kg)	rice noodles	10 lb (4 kg)
1 lb (500 g)	peanuts, chopped coarsely	4 lb (2 kg)
2 bunches	cilantro, chopped	6 bunches
1 large bunch	radishes, sliced thinly	4 bunches

Soften the tamarind pulp with enough warm water to make it a thick liquid. Press on the pulp with your hands or a wooden spoon. Strain out the seeds and reserve the liquid. You should have about 1/3 cup (1 ½ cups for the larger recipe).

Squeeze the limes. You will need ¾ cup juice (3 cups for the larger recipe).

Add the tamarind and the lime juice to the sugar, fish sauce, and the 'sauce for chicken'. Mix well and store covered in the refrigerator. This can be made a day or two in advance.

Steam or boil the vegetables until barely tender. Drain and mix in the minced garlic, the garlic chili paste, and the sliced scallions. Set aside.

In a large plastic tub or bowl, pour boiling water over the noodles. Let soak a few minutes until softened. Drain and rinse with cold water. Cut in 5-inch lengths, using scissors. Cover lightly. These preceding steps may be done several hours in advance.

To serve, bring sauce ingredients to a boil and add about 2/3 of the chopped peanuts. Mix thoroughly. Add the sauce and the vegetables to the noodles and mix thoroughly. Let cool to room temperature.

Before serving, add the remaining peanuts, the chopped cilantro, and the radishes to the noodles and toss lightly to combine.

*Note: for a completely vegetarian pad Thai, substitute tamari or light soy sauce for the fish sauce.

Wine suggestions: medium to full-bodied white; Chardonnay, Muscat, Gewürztraminer

Provençal Onion and Tomato Tart

This onion tart can be served as a main course or an appetizer. Once the ingredients are prepared, the pies can be put together quickly, assembly-line style. It is best served warm but also perfectly fine at room temperature. Be sure not to use too much cheese, as it tends to make a heavy layer that is hard to cut through with a fork.

For 25 servings		For 100 servings
4	ready-to-bake tart shells	16
5 lb (2 ½ kg)	onions, thickly sliced	20 lb (9 kg)
½ C (125 ml)	olive oil, approximately	2 C (500 ml)
2 Tb	sugar	8 Tb
2 tsp	salt	3 Tb
1 tsp	pepper	1 Tb
1 lb (500 g)	Gruyere or Swiss cheese, grated	4 lb (2 kg)
2 ½ lb (1 kg)	Roma tomatoes, quartered	9 lb (4 kg)
1 lb (500 g)	black oil-cured olives, pitted	4 lb (2 kg)
1 Tb	fresh thyme leaves	4 Tb

Preheat the oven to 425 F. Pre-bake the tart shells by lining each with aluminum foil. Press the foil firmly against the pastry and prick it with a fork. Bake for 10 minutes. The pastry should begin to look flaky and opaque. Remove the foil and cook for 5 more minutes or until the pastry is very lightly browned. Let cool.

Heat a layer of olive oil in a large frying pan and add the onions. Sprinkle with some sugar, salt, and pepper. Sauté the onions slowly, stirring from time to time until they are soft and well browned. Do this step in batches as necessary.

Line up the pie shells and distribute a layer of onions, followed by a layer of cheese. Finish with a layer of tomatoes, skin sides up, placed close together and radiating from the center. Scatter about ½ cup of olives over each tart. Drizzle a fine thread of olive oil over all tarts.

Bake in a moderately hot (350 F) oven for 40 minutes or until very hot throughout and the tomatoes have cooked through. To serve, cut each pie into 8 slices.

Wine suggestions: dry whites; Riesling or Sauvignon Blanc.

Three Cheese Baked Penne

Vegetarians and non-vegetarians alike love this homey baked pasta dish. Economical to make, the pasta and sauce can be prepared ahead of time and then combined and heated through just before serving. Be sure not to over-bake, as it will become dry.

For 25 servings		For 100 servings
5 lb (2 ½ kg)	penne	18 lb (8 kg)
1 dozen	eggs	4 dozen
1 qt (1 L)	crème fraîche (see recipe p.151) or cream	4 qt (4 L)
1 lb (500 g)	Feta cheese, crumbled	4 lb (2 kg)
1 lb (500 g)	Swiss cheese, grated	4 lb (2 kg)
¾ lb (750 g)	Parmesan cheese, grated	3 lb (1 ½ kg)
2 tsp	oregano	2 Tb
½ bunch	parsley, chopped	2 bunches
	salt and pepper	

Cook 2 to 3 pounds of penne at a time in plenty of boiling salted water. When barely tender or at the 'al dente' point, immediately drain the pasta into a colander. Plunge the colander into a sink of cold water or run cold water over until the pasta has cooled down. Drain well and put the cooked pasta into greased roasting or baking pans.

In a very large bowl, beat the eggs until frothy. Add the crème fraîche, cheeses, and herbs. Season generously with salt and pepper. Distribute the sauce between the pans of penne and stir to combine. Bake lightly covered with foil in a moderate oven (325 F) about 30 minutes.

Wine suggestions: dry whites; Riesling, Sauvignon Blanc, Pinot Gris.

SIDE DISHES

I still smile at the memory of opening Jim's book Thanks for Coming, *discovering inside the 1966 article "Who's Who in the London Underground" and seeing the photo of Jim Haynes, ranked just ahead of the Beatles. How cool is that?*

Jake Lamar, author

BREADS and GRAINS

Cornbread

Good enough to eat on its own and a perfect accompaniment for chili con carne, this American classic wows European guests chez Jim Haynes.

For 25 servings		For 100 servings
8 C (1 kg)	flour	30 C (3 ¾ kg)
4 C (600 g)	cornmeal	15 C (2 ¼ kg)
1 Tb	salt	4 Tb
1 ½ C (300 g)	sugar	6 C (1 ¼ kg)
5 Tb	baking powder	1 ¼ C (250 g)
8	eggs	30
7 C (1 ¾ L)	buttermilk	7 qt (7 L)
10 oz (300 g)	butter, melted	2 ½ lb (1 ¼ kg)

Mix all dry ingredients. In a separate large bowl, beat together eggs, buttermilk and butter. Stir into dry ingredients until just combined.

Turn the batter into 2 (9 x 13-inch) greased pans (use 6 pans for 100 servings) and bake in a moderate oven (325 F) for about 30 minutes. For the larger recipe, you will have two or three rounds of baking. Keep the batter refrigerated between bakings.

Cut into squares for serving.

Garlic Bread

Everyone loves garlic bread. This recipe makes a few pieces per person and can easily be doubled or tripled. If you can find it, high quality, artisanal bread, although expensive, makes a big difference in taste.

For 25 servings		For 100 servings
3	French or sour dough baguettes	12
2 Tb	garlic, chopped	½ C (2 heads)
8 oz (250 g)	butter, softened	2 lb (1 kg)
5 sprigs	parsley, finely chopped	2 bunches
4 Tb	Parmesan cheese, grated (optional)	½ lb (250 g)

Cut each baguette in half. With each of the halves, cut 1-inch slices but do not go all the way through. Mix the garlic, butter, and parsley together. Spread a teaspoon or two of the butter mixture between each slice. If desired, sprinkle with Parmesan cheese. Wrap the baguette halves in foil tightly. To serve, heat for 5 to 10 minutes in a moderate oven (325 F). Can be prepared early, refrigerated, and heated at the last minute.

Garlic Toasts

Crispy garlic toasts are a great accompaniment with soups, stews, and salads. The following method is messy but fast and produces a large quantity of crispy toasts for soups or dips. You can flavor the olive oil with a few tablespoons dried herbs such as thyme or rosemary or even a strip of orange peel for more pronounced flavor. Make these a few days in advance if desired but be sure to store in tightly covered containers.

For 25 servings		For 100 servings
2	baguettes	8
½ C (125 ml)	olive oil, approximately	2 C (500 ml)
2 large	garlic cloves, whole, smashed	4 large
	Optional flavorings: strip of orange peel, branch of thyme or rosemary	

Slice the baguettes into thin rounds. There will be approximately 35 to 40 pieces per baguette. Line up several baking sheets and arrange the slices on them. Bake in a warm oven (300 F) for about 10 to15 minutes just to dry out the bread but not brown it. Remove from oven.

Place the olive oil and garlic in a medium-sized bowl and microwave on high for about 1 minute to warm the oil. Add any flavorings at this time. Working quickly, dip each bread slice into the olive oil/garlic mixture and place back onto the baking sheet. Add more oil, warming it if necessary. Do not allow the bread to become saturated.

Bake for 10 to 15 minutes in a moderate oven (325 F) or until lightly browned. Cool and cover tightly until serving time

Basic Long-Grain Rice

For 25 servings		For 100 servings
4 lb (1 ¾ kg)	long grain rice	14 lb (6 kg)
4 Tb	cooking oil	8 oz (250 ml)
4 Tb	butter	8 oz (250 ml)
1 Tb	salt	4 Tb

Using a large pitcher, measuring cup or other container, measure out the rice and note the amount. You will need double this amount of water. Bring water to a boil.

In a very large pot, heat the oil and butter together until sizzling. Add the rice, stirring to coat well, and heat through. Add the boiling water, stir briefly, and bring the mixture to a boil. Add salt. Lower the heat to a simmer, cover, and cook for 20 minutes or until the water is absorbed and the rice is tender.

Variations:
Vegetable or chicken broth may replace the water (omit the salt).

Saffron or turmeric may be added with the water. Use 1 teaspoon turmeric per pound of rice or a large pinch of saffron.

Peas, diced tomato or carrot, fresh herbs, or finely chopped shallot may be added as flavoring at the end of the cooking time. Per pound of rice, use ½ cup each of peas, tomato or carrot and ¼ cup fresh herbs or shallots.

Basmati Rice

Soft and delicate, basmati rice takes less water and less time to cook than long grain rice but it must be rinsed before cooking. With sautéed onions, it is called Butter Rice when it accompanies spicy Indian dishes. Jasmine rice, Thai rice with a subtle nutty flavor, is cooked in the same manner

For 25 servings		For 100 servings
4 lb (1 ¾ kg)	basmati rice	14 lb (6 kg)
4 Tb	butter	½ lb (250 g)
3	onions, finely chopped	3 lb (1 ½ kg)
1 Tb	salt	4 Tb

Using a large pitcher, measuring cup, or other container, measure out the rice and note the amount. You will need 1 ½ times this amount of water to rice. Bring water to a boil.

In a large sieve, rinse the rice thoroughly with cold water. In a very large pot, melt butter and cook onions until softened and translucent. Add rice, stirring thoroughly to coat all the grains. Add salt and pour in the boiling water. Stir well, cover and bring to boil. Turn heat to low and cook undisturbed for 10 minutes. Test a few grains, cooking a few minutes more if necessary.

Basic Pasta

Keeping pasta warm, moist and flavorful for a crowd requires some special handling. This is one method that works. Be sure not to overcook the pasta and avoid very fine pastas such as thin spaghetti, which will get too soft.

For 25 servings		For 100 servings
5 lb (2 ½ kg)	pasta (such as bucatini, farfalle, fusilli, penne or rigatoni)	18 lb (8 kg)
1 C (250 ml)	olive oil, approximately	1 qt (1 L)
	salt and pepper	
	Optional:	
1 small bunch	parsley, chopped	3 bunches
1 ½ Tb	dried oregano or herbes de Provence	6 Tb
1 Tb	garlic, finely chopped	¼ C (1 head)

Cook 2 to 3 pounds of pasta at a time in plenty of boiling salted water. Taste and stop the cooking just at the point where the pasta is 'al dente' or barely tender. Immediately, drain the pasta into a colander. Plunge the colander into a sink of cold water or run cold water over until the pasta has cooled down. Drain well.

Put the pasta into large baking pans and toss with enough olive oil to coat the pasta. This will keep the pasta from becoming sticky. Season generously with salt, pepper, and mix in herbs and garlic as desired. Cover lightly with foil. The pasta may be set aside at this point for a few hours.

At serving time, heat in a warm oven (300 F) for about 10 minutes. Do not overbake.

Fragrant Couscous

Plain or with the 'fragrant' seasoning below, couscous is well appreciated by guests. Couscous is easy to prepare with this caveat: do not add too much liquid or the grains will stick together like paste. Most commercially sold couscous is pre-cooked and the amount of added liquid varies depending on the brand.

For 25 servings		For 100 servings
4 lb (1 ½ kg)	couscous	14 lb (6 kg)
	water or broth (vegetable or chicken)	
1-2	onions, chopped	4
4 oz (125 g)	butter	1 lb (500 g)
3	cardamom pods	12
2 Tb	cumin	4 Tb
1 Tb	cinnamon	2 Tb
1 tsp	cayenne	1 Tb
1 Tb	salt (or to taste)	4 Tb
½ C (50 g)	garam masala (optional)	2 C (200 g)
½ bunch	parsley, chopped	2 bunches
½ bunch	mint, chopped	2 bunches

Using a large pitcher, measuring cup, or other container, measure out the couscous and note the amount. You will need 1 ½ times this amount of water or broth. Bring the liquid to a boil. Be sure to check the package instructions to confirm the amount of liquid needed.

Divide the couscous between 2 or more large bowls and add the hot liquid in equal portions. Mix thoroughly and let stand lightly covered for about 15 minutes.

In a frying pan, sauté the onions until soft. Add the spices and optional masala to the pan and heat until fragrant but take care not to burn. Add to the couscous.

Add the chopped herbs just before serving. Couscous can be served hot or at room temperature.

VEGETABLES

Asparagus Vinaigrette with Pink Onions

Even in season, asparagus is not cheap but if you want to delight your guests, this is a lovely spring treat. The asparagus can be cooked in advance but add the vinaigrette just before serving or the asparagus will turn yellow. Sieved hard boiled egg and ribbons of pink pickled onions make this a colorful and elegant dish to accompany the main course or as a starter.

For 25 servings		For 100 servings
7 lb (3 kg)	asparagus	25 lb (11 kg)
	salt and pepper	
	Basic I or II Vinaigrette (see recipes pp.53 and 54)	
	Optional:	
	Pink Onions (see recipe p.123)	
4	eggs, hard-boiled	12

Fill one or two large pots with water and bring to a full boil. Add about 2 tablespoons of salt to each pot.

Wash the asparagus and snap off the ends just at the point where they easily break. Cook the asparagus in batches (about 2 pounds per batch) removing each to a large bowl (or sink) full of ice cold water as soon as it is tender, about 7 to 8 minutes.

Drain the asparagus and pat dry with towels. Store in large flat pans covered with a damp towel and plastic wrap until serving time.

The vinaigrette can be prepared a day or two in advance and refrigerated. To serve, uncover the asparagus one pan at a time and season with salt and pepper. Drizzle some of the vinaigrette over the top and turn gently to coat all spears. Chop the hard-boiled eggs finely or push through a sieve.

For served plates, place 3 to 5 spears on each small plate, add a small clump of the pink onions and sprinkle each serving with a little of the sieved hard-boiled egg. For buffet serving, arrange the asparagus on 1 or 2 large platters and decorate with the pink onions and sieved egg. Refill the platters as needed.

Baked and Unbaked Tomatoes

Hot or cold, tomatoes are easy to prepare for a crowd. In season and fresh from the garden or a local market, tomatoes need little to dress them up. Just be sure not to store tomatoes in the refrigerator: it spoils their taste and texture. Once you have prepared the tomatoes, leave them in their pans for easy serving. Baked tomatoes go well with stews and spicy dishes. Unbaked, tomatoes are a welcomed side dish at a Mediterranean buffet with other salads, fish, and meat dishes.

For 25 servings		For 100 servings
15	tomatoes, cut in halves	50
	coarse salt and pepper	
4 Tb	butter	½ lb (250 g)
	Or	
4 Tb	olive oil	1 C (250 ml)
	Optional:	
15 sprigs	mixed fresh herbs, finely chopped	2 bunches
	(parsley, tarragon, chives, basil or chervil)	

Arrange the tomato halves cut side up on baking pans.

For Baked Tomatoes: Sprinkle with salt, pepper, dot with butter, and the optional herbs. Bake in a moderate oven (325 F) until just softened about 15 minutes. May be done a few hours in advance and reheated in a warm oven.

For Unbaked Tomatoes: Sprinkle with salt, pepper, and the optional herbs, and drizzle with olive oil about ½ hour before serving.

Variation: Balsamic vinaigrette (see recipe p.55) can be substituted for the olive oil.

Jim's Glazed Carrots

Sweet and Southern (like Jim), this is less of a recipe and more of an engineering marvel. Jim Haynes somehow perfected a method of packing a large pot with row after row of carrots, standing on top of each other, end to end. Once that's done, the rest is easy. This makes a good Thanksgiving dish.

For 25 servings		For 100 servings
7 lb (3 kg)	carrots, peeled	25 lb (11 kg)
¾ lb (375 g)	light brown sugar	3 lb (1 ½ kg)
4 oz (125 g)	butter, unsalted	1 lb (500 g)
1-2	cinnamon sticks	5
	salt and pepper	
	water	

Slice the carrots into julienne strips about 3 inches long and ½ wide. They will not all be the same shape but try to make them the same length and do not cut them too thinly or they will become too soft when cooked.

Now, for the engineering part. In the large pot, (it can be a tall-sided pot or a broad one), stack the carrots in bunches on end. Continue this process until the bottom of the pot is covered with a tight row of carrots. Sprinkle with salt and pepper. Repeat with a second row on top of the first. Continue in this manner until all the carrots are tightly packed in the pot. You may find it easier to lay the pot on its side while stacking the layers. There should be about 3 or 4 inches remaining at the top.

Add enough water to the pot to cover the carrots. Place the butter, sugar, cinnamon sticks, and a generous spoonful of salt and pepper on top of the carrots. Bring the contents to a boil. This will take quite some time. Immediately turn off the heat. Keep the pot covered, leaving the carrots to cook as they cool. They can simply sit there stewing in their juices for several hours until serving time. Reheat briefly.

Hare Masale ki Sem (Green Beans with Ginger & Cilantro)

These flavorful beans can be made hours ahead of your party. To save preparation time, frozen green beans are a good substitute for fresh ones. The fresh green chiles are an important part of this dish. Add a lot or a little depending on your tolerance for spicy food.

For 25 servings		For 100 servings
8 lb (4 kg)	green beans	27 lb (12 kg)
1 (6-inch) piece	ginger, peeled	4 (6-inch) pieces
1 C (250 ml)	cooking oil, approximately	2 C (500 ml)
1 Tb	black mustard seeds	4 Tb
4 Tb	cumin, ground	1 C (120 g)
1½ tsp	turmeric, ground	2 Tb
1 Tb	salt (or to taste)	4 Tb
3–6	hot green chili peppers, finely chopped	10–15
½ C (2 lemons)	lemon juice	2 C (8 lemons)
2 C (500 ml)	water or chicken broth	2 qt (2 L)
2 bunches	cilantro	6 bunches

Trim the beans and cut into 1-inch pieces. Cut the ginger first into very thin slices and then, into thin strips.

Heat about ¼ inch of oil in a large pot on medium-high heat. Add the mustard seeds and fry until they pop. Add the ginger and stir continuously for a matter of seconds. Add the green beans and toss well. Add cumin, turmeric, salt, and chili peppers and stir thoroughly. For the larger recipe, you may have to do this in 2 batches.

Add lemon juice and water or broth and bring to simmer. Cover, turn heat low, and simmer gently for 10 minutes. If using frozen beans, add only half the liquid and simmer for 5 minutes only. Stir in the chopped cilantro, cover, and cook about 1 minute longer. Serve hot or at room temperature.

Makhani Dal

Almost every Indian dinner is accompanied by some form of dal. Split peas, dried beans or lentils are the basis of dal, which then is seasoned and flavored in myriad ways. Makhani dal is a very versatile and popular recipe with spices and cream. Canned lentils work well and make this dish extremely easy to prepare.

For 25 servings		For 100 servings
½ lb (250 g)	butter	2 lb (1 kg)
½ C (125 ml)	olive oil	2 C (500 ml)
2 Tb	garlic, chopped	½ C (2 heads)
2 Tb	ginger, grated	1 (8-inch) piece
2 heaping tsp	chili powder	3 Tb
4 lb (1 ¾ kg)	canned lentils	14 lb (6 kg)
1 can	tomato purée (29 oz/765 g)	4 cans
15 sprigs	cilantro	2 bunches
	salt and pepper	
2 C (500 ml)	cream, approximately	2 qt (2 L)

Heat olive oil and butter in large heavy pan and fry the garlic, ginger, and chili powder for about 5 minutes. Add the lentils and tomato purée, stirring well.

Separate the cilantro leaves from the stalks and chop both separately. Add the chopped stalks to the lentils, season to taste with salt and pepper, then leave to simmer over low heat about 15 minutes.

Before serving, stir in the chopped cilantro leaves and enough cream to make a thick consistency. Can be served warm or at room temperature.

Masoor Dal

This is one of the most widely eaten dals in India. It is simple to make, delicious to eat, and an important accompaniment to any Indian dinner.

For 25 servings		For 100 servings
2 ½ lb (1 kg)	pale red split lentils	9 lb (4 kg)
2 ½ qt (2 ½ L)	water	10 qt (10 L)
1-inch piece	ginger, unpeeled	4-inch piece
1 heaping tsp	turmeric	5 tsp
	salt	
¼ lb (125 g)	butter	1 lb (500 g)
1 Tb	cumin seeds	10 tsp
1 Tb	coriander, ground	10 tsp
1 scant tsp	cayenne (or to taste)	1 Tb
1 bunch	cilantro, chopped	3 bunches

Bring lentils and water to the boil in a very large pot and remove any scum that collects on the surface. Turn down to a simmer and add ginger and turmeric. Stir, cover, and simmer for about 2 hours. Check frequently, stirring to avoid sticking on the bottom of the pan. When the lentils are tender, remove the ginger, and add salt to taste.

In a frying pan, melt the butter over medium heat and when hot add the cumin seeds. Allow to sizzle and add the ground coriander and cayenne pepper. Pour this butter mixture into the lentils and stir well.

Serve warm or at room temperature sprinkled with the finely chopped fresh cilantro.

Mary's Favorite Potato Gratin

In French, "gratin" means a top crust made with crumbs or cheese. What makes this dish fabulous is the sim-mered broth, herbs, and milk mixture. Cream makes an even more unctuous gratin.

For 25 servings		For 100 servings
6 lb (2 ½ kg)	baking potatoes, peeled	22 lb (10 kg)
2	garlic cloves, smashed	6
3 Tb	butter, softened	¾ lb (375 g)
1 ½ C (375 ml)	whole milk or cream	1 ½ qt (1 ½ L)
1 ½ C (375 ml)	chicken or beef broth	1 ½ qt (1 ½ L)
1 small sprig	rosemary	2 sprigs
1 sprig	thyme	5 sprigs
1	bay leaf	4
½ tsp	nutmeg	2 tsp
2 ½ tsp	salt	2 Tb
1 scant tsp	pepper	1 Tb
½ lb (250 g)	Parmesan cheese, grated	2 lb (1 kg)
½ lb (250 g)	Gruyere cheese, grated	2 lb (1 kg)

Slice the potatoes into 1/8 inch slices (by hand, food processor, Japanese slicer, or mandolin). Put them into cold water. This step can be done early in the day.

Prepare 1 large roasting pan (use 4 pans for 100 servings) by rubbing some of the smashed garlic on the inside of the pan, then, buttering the pan with a tablespoon of butter.

Put the remaining garlic in a saucepan and add the milk or cream, broth, rosemary, thyme, and bay leaves. Bring to a boil, reduce heat, and let simmer for 15 minutes. Remove the herbs and garlic and set aside.

Mix the salt, pepper, and nutmeg together in a small bowl. Combine the cheeses in a bowl. Drain the potatoes and pat dry with towels. Cover bottom of each pan with a layer of the potato slices. Sprinkle lightly with the salt mixture and follow with about a cup of the cheese. Continue layering in this manner ending with cheese on the top. Add the broth and milk mixture. With a spatula (or clean hands), press down hard on top of the gratin to compact it. Dot with the remaining butter. Once prepared, the gratin can sit at room temperature for an hour or two before baking. For the larger recipe, unless your oven is a professional size, you will have two rounds of baking.

Bake the gratin for about an hour in a moderately hot oven (375 F), until the top is brown and crusty and a knife cuts easily through potatoes. Cool the dish for about 15 minutes before serving and cut into squares. Can be kept warm in a turned off warm oven, uncovered, for about 40 minutes.

Puffed Baked Potato Halves

Well, they don't always puff but mostly, they do. This is a baked potato for a crowd: incredibly easy to prepare and tasty as is. Potatoes are best eaten once cooked so they cannot be baked too far in advance. However, the preparation time is so short that working quickly, you can get these in the oven in no time. Be sure to select baking potatoes that are not too large, keep the heat high, and do not skimp on the coarse salt.

For 25 servings		For 100 servings
14	baking potatoes, medium-sized	50
	coarse salt	

Preheat the oven to 450 F. Scrub the potatoes and cut in halves lengthwise. Arrange the halves, cut side up, on a baking sheet. One baking sheet will fit about 25 halves. For 100 servings, if your oven only can fit 2 or 3 trays, prepare what can be baked at one time and then repeat the process.

Sprinkle generously with coarse salt. Bake for 40 minutes or until the tops are browned and puffed. Test by plunging a knife through the center of one to determine doneness. Serve within the hour. They may stay in a turned-off warm oven but do not cover them.

Parsley Potatoes

With a flavorful stew, the simplest potato dish is the best. Cook the potatoes as close to serving time as possible and to preserve the freshest taste, do not cover.

For 25 servings		For 100 servings
7 lb (3 kg)	small boiling potatoes, peeled if necessary	28 lb (12 kg)
4 oz (125 g)	butter, melted	1 lb (500 g)
1 bunch	parsley, chopped	4 bunches
	salt and pepper	

If small new potatoes with thin skins are available, there is no need to peel them. Otherwise, potatoes can be peeled the day before and left in cold water to cover.

Using one or two large pots, cover with cold water, adding about 1 tablespoon of salt per pound of potato, and bring to a boil. Cook about 15 to 20 minutes or until the potatoes can just be pierced with a knife. Drain.

Arrange in shallow baking pans. Combine butter, parsley, salt, and pepper and pour over the potatoes, stirring gently. Taste for seasoning. Keep in a warm oven (250 F), uncovered, until ready to serve.

Spinach with Artichokes

One of the most popular dinners at Jim Haynes's atelier is Thanksgiving. An elbow-to-elbow international crowd shows up every year to take part in the traditional American feast. This spinach and artichoke recipe is a practical side dish because it can be prepared largely in advance and heated through at the last minute, thus minimizing stovetop use. The water chestnuts aren't essential but they add a nice little crunch.

For 25 servings		For 100 servings
1	onion, diced	4
2 lb (1 kg)	frozen artichoke hearts	8 lb (4 kg)
4 oz (125 g)	butter	1 lb (500 g)
6 lb (2 ½ kg)	frozen leaf spinach	22 lb (10 kg)
3 C (750 ml)	crème fraîche (see recipe p.151) or cream	3 qt (3 L)
2 tsp	nutmeg	3 Tb
	salt and pepper	
	Optional:	
1 lb (500 g)	sliced water chestnuts, drained	4 lb (2 kg)

Let the artichoke hearts defrost about 1 hour and then cut them into thick slices. In a large pot, melt the butter and add the diced onions. Sauté gently until the onions are soft. Add the artichokes. Stir gently and simmer just until the hearts are heated through. Season with salt and pepper and set aside.

Cook the spinach briefly in the microwave just to defrost and heat up. Do not add additional water. Do this in batches, using a glass bowl covered with plastic film, allowing an air space. Do not overcook the spinach, as it must be reheated later. As each hot batch of spinach is ready, place it in a large colander over a bowl to drain off any accumulated water. Transfer the spinach to a large pot.

Add the nutmeg, salt, and pepper. Check the seasoning carefully, adding more nutmeg if desired. Fold in the artichokes and the (optional) water chestnuts.

At serving time, add the cream, heat gently, and stir carefully to avoid breaking the artichokes. Check the seasoning once more. The best way to keep the spinach hot is to create a bain-marie or double boiler by putting the pot into a larger pot, partly filled with hot water. Keeping the spinach from the direct heat will avoid scorching and overcooking.

Palak Bhajee (Spicy Spinach)

This spinach recipe is a fine addition to an Indian menu. Using frozen spinach is strongly recommended, as it will make this dish a snap to prepare. Bear in mind that the amount of fresh spinach for one hundred servings would practically fill a room. As with many Indian dishes, palak bhajee can be served at room temperature.

For 25 servings		For 100 servings
8 Tb (125 g)	butter	1 lb (500 g)
6 Tb	olive oil	12 oz (375 ml)
2 Tb	cumin seeds	8 Tb
6	onions, chopped	4 lb (2 kg)
1 (4-inch) piece	ginger, peeled and cut in strips	4 (4-inch) pieces
½ C (2 heads)	garlic, chopped	2 C (8 heads)
1 Tb	cumin, ground	4 Tb
1 Tb	coriander, ground	4 Tb
1 Tb	turmeric	4 Tb
2 tsp	chili powder	2 ½ Tb
2 Tb	salt	8 Tb
7 lb (3 kg)	frozen leaf spinach	25 lb (12 kg)

In a large pot, heat the butter with the oil until sizzling and fry the cumin seeds about 30 seconds. Stir in the onions and fry over high heat, stirring until golden, about 10 minutes.

Add the ginger and garlic and fry a few minutes. Stir in the ground cumin, coriander, turmeric, chili powder, and salt. Add the spinach and stir rapidly until well combined. Add a small amount of water if the mixture seems dry. Cover and cook gently about 5 minutes or until the spinach is tender.

Taste for seasoning, adding salt and chili powder if needed.

Ratatouille

In the most delicate recipes for ratatouille, each vegetable is separately sautéed in olive oil and then carefully combined with the tomatoes. This is a long process when cooking a large quantity. In this recipe, there is less sautéeing (and a lot less oil) but it is a very flavorful dish. The important thing to remember is not to overcook this vegetable stew, as it will become mushy. Add fresh basil just before serving. This is an excellent make-ahead dish.

For 25 servings		For 100 servings
3 lb (1 ½ kg)	eggplant, cut in 1-inch cubes	12 lb (5 ½ kg)
1 C (250 ml)	olive oil, approximately	1 qt (1 L)
2 Tb	garlic, chopped	½ C (2 heads)
8	onions, chopped	8 lb (4 kg)
3	green peppers, coarsely chopped	12
3 lb (1 ½ kg)	zucchini, sliced	12 lb (5 ½ kg)
1 ½ cans	tomatoes, chopped (29 oz/765 g)	6 cans
	salt and pepper	
1 bunch	parsley, finely chopped	4 bunches
1 bunch	basil, chopped	4 bunches

Generously salt the cubed eggplant and set aside in a large bowl or colander about 1 hour to draw out the liquid.

Using a very large pot, heat about ¼ inch of olive oil and sauté the garlic and onions until softened. For the larger recipe, use two pots as necessary and divide the ingredients between the two.

Drain the eggplant and add to the onions. Season with pepper and drizzle with olive oil. Add the green peppers followed by the zucchini and tomatoes, seasoning each layer generously with salt, pepper, and olive oil.

Bring to a simmer, lower the heat and cook stirring very gently from time to time until all the vegetables are just tender, about 30 minutes. Add the parsley. Bear in mind that with large quantities, the vegetables will continue to cook after the heat is turned off.

At serving time, add the basil and taste for seasoning, adding more salt and pepper as necessary. May be served hot or at room temperature.

CONDIMENTS

Cucumber Raita

What's cool as a cucumber? Raita, a yogurt relish, that is a staple at an Indian dinner. A cool contrast with spicy food, yogurt relish is served as a condiment or as a complete dish. The following recipe allows a small "condiment size" serving per person and can be doubled easily for larger portions.

For 25 servings		For 100 servings
1	English cucumber, peeled and diced	4
3 C (750 ml)	plain yogurt	3 qt (3 L)
4	onions, finely chopped	4 lb (2 kg)
	salt and pepper	

Combine the diced cucumber, onions, and yogurt. Season with salt and pepper to taste. Refrigerate 1 to 2 hours before serving. Can be made a day ahead.

Mint Chutney

Fresh mint chutney is a natural with curries but also tasty with meat and fish. Once the apples and onions are peeled, this condiment is a snap to finish using a blender or food processor. It is best prepared the day you use it.

For 25 servings		For 100 servings
1 lb (500 g)	hard cooking apples or green mangoes	4 lb (2 kg)
3	onions	3 lb (1 ¾ kg)
1 bunch	mint, leaves only	4 bunches
1 C (200 g)	sugar	4 C (800 g)
	salt and cayenne pepper

Peel and core the apples and chop coarsely. If using mangoes, peel and cut away the fruit from the pit. Peel and coarsely chop the onions.

Use a blender to chop up the fruit in batches, adding the onions, mint, and sugar. Add salt and a little cayenne to taste. Do not over blend the mixture: it should be chunky.

Mango, Apple and Apricot Chutney

The chutney family is a diverse group with a lot of personality. They can be made with almost any fruit, using vinegar and sugar for the sweet sour effect. In this one, apple is the tender underpinning, bumped up with as much cayenne pepper as desired. This can be made well in advance and stored in jars.

For 25 servings		For 100 servings
1 lb (500 g)	hard green apples	4 lb (2 kg)
2	firm mangos	8
2 Tb	garlic, finely chopped	½ C (2 heads)
2-inch piece	ginger, peeled	8-inch piece
1 C (150 g)	golden raisins	1 lb (500 g)
6 oz (200 g)	dried apricots	1 ½ lb (750 g)
2 C (500 ml)	white wine vinegar	2 qt (2 L)
2 C (400 g)	sugar	8 C (1600 g)
	salt and cayenne pepper	

Peel and core the apples and chop coarsely. Peel the mangoes and cut away the fruit from the pit. Crush the garlic cloves and ginger with a heavy knife or rolling pin.

Mix all the ingredients together in a heavy-bottomed pan and bring to the boil. Turn down the heat and stir frequently until mixture thickens (about 45 minutes).

When thick, turn off the heat and allow to cool. It will thicken more on cooling. Store in covered containers in a cool place.

Pink Onions

These pickled onions turn progressively pinker the longer they remain in their brine, especially if pieces of the very dark red outer skin are added to the mixture. Perfect with asparagus, these versatile onions are also excellent with steak, roast pork, cold meats or grilled vegetables.

For 25 servings		For 100 servings
3	red onions, peeled	10
1 ½ tsp	sugar	5 tsp
1 ½ tsp	salt	5 tsp
1 C (250 ml)	white wine vinegar	1 qt (1 L)
1 tsp	pepper	1 Tb

Use a mandolin, food processor, Japanese slicer, or a very sharp knife to slice the onions into very thin rounds.

Mix salt, pepper, sugar, and vinegar in a large bowl. Put onion slices in a large colander and set it in the sink. Bring a kettle of water to a boil and pour the water over the onions. Put the warm onions into vinegar mixture and add enough cold water to cover. Let stand until onions are pink, about 30 minutes or longer for more color. Stir from time to time.

Refrigerate until serving time. Pink onions keep for a long time in the refrigerator.

DESSERTS

My policy is to try to never say the word no.

Jim Haynes

I did not get the question but the answer is Yes.

Timothy Leary

CAKES, COOKIES, and PIES

Baking is a real pleasure for many home cooks. But eight cakes? It is a challenge, especially with a standard home oven. In the following recipes, the trick is to allow time for more than one round of baking and use very large mixing bowls. Cake batter will hold up well in the refrigerator between bakings if you use fresh double-acting baking powder. Baking in quantity is good exercise! Most electric mixers will not hold enough ingredients to be useful so you'll want to have plenty of hands to help with the stirring. Most ovens will accommodate four cakes at a time. To facilitate serving, sheet cakes and pies can be left in their pans. Making cakes ahead and serving them with a sauce or a topping is another way to manage large quantities. If oven space is really too limited, an unbaked cake such as the Strawberry Refrigerator Cheesecake, is an excellent choice.

Carrot Cake

Credit the healthy, hippy 1970s for this American favorite. International guests at Jim's Paris parties immediately took to carrot cake even though there was some confusion over a dessert made with carrots and frosted with cheese. This is a cake for any time of the year and can be baked several days in advance.

For 25 servings (2 cakes)		For 100 servings (8 cakes)
4 C (800 g)	sugar	16 C (3200 g)
8	eggs	32
2 C (500 ml)	oil, canola or safflower	2 qt (2 L)
2 ½ tsp	vanilla	3 Tb
4 C (500 g)	flour	16 C (2 kg)
4 tsp	baking powder	5 Tb
2 tsp	salt	8 tsp
2 tsp	cinnamon	8 tsp
2 lb (1 kg)	carrots, grated	8 lb (4 kg)
2 C (300 g)	nuts, chopped	2 ½ lb (1 kg)
	Optional:	
2 ½ C (375 g)	raisins	3 ½ lb (1 ½ kg)

Beat the sugar and eggs together until well blended. Stir in the oil and vanilla. In a separate bowl, mix the flour, baking soda, salt, and cinnamon. Combine with the egg mixture. Fold in carrots, nuts, and raisins.

Divide the batter between 2 (9 x 13-inch) greased baking pans. For the larger recipe, use 8 pans for 100 servings and make two at a time. Refrigerate the batter between baking times. Bake the cakes in a moderately hot oven (350 F) for approximately 40 minutes. Let cool completely.

Frost with cream cheese frosting. The cakes may be left in the pans for ease of serving.

Cream Cheese Frosting

For 25 servings   For 100 servings

8 oz (250 g)	cream cheese	2 lb (1 kg)
5 oz (200 g)	butter	1 ¼ lb (625 g)
1 ½ lb (750 g)	powdered sugar	6 lb (3 kg)
1 ½ tsp	vanilla	2 Tb

Bring the cream cheese and butter to room temperature. Cream the two together until smooth. Add sugar gradually, shaking it through a strainer to get rid of the lumps and beat until smooth. Add the vanilla. Cover and refrigerate until it has a good spreading consistency.

Variation: Ginger Cream Cheese Frosting

Add 1 tablespoon (¼ cup for the larger recipe) fresh grated ginger to the frosting.

Taste and add more ginger, if desired.

Chocolate Cake with Armagnac (Gâteau au Chocolat à l'Armagnac)

This elegant dessert straight from the heart of the Gers region of France combines the prunes of Agen and the grape brandy Armagnac for which the area is justly famous. This cake is not difficult to put together but it cannot be baked in large pans. This means that the baking must be done four cakes at a time (unless you have access to large ovens). Cut each cake into very thin servings, as it is quite rich. Serve with its sauce of crème fraîche and the Armagnac-soaked prunes.

For 25 servings (2 cakes)		For 100 servings (8 cakes)
1 ½ lb (750 g)	prunes, pitted	6 lb (3 kg)
1 ¼ C (300 ml)	water	5 C (1 ¼ L)
1 ½ C (375 ml)	Armagnac	2 bottles (1.5 L)
14 oz (400 g)	dark bittersweet chocolate	3 ½ lb (1600 g)
1 C (250 g)	butter	2 lb (1 kg)
8	eggs	32
1 C (200 g)	sugar	4 C (800 g)

The night before, put the prunes and water in a saucepan and bring almost to the boil. Pour into a bowl. While still warm, add 1 ¼ cups (5 cups for 100 servings) of the Armagnac. Soak, lightly covered, overnight in the refrigerator.

Break up the chocolate and place in a Pyrex or ceramic bowl with the butter. Heat this mixture in the oven or microwave until it is just melted, checking and stirring frequently. Cool and add 2 tablespoons (8 tablespoons for the larger recipe) of Armagnac.

Separate the eggs and set the whites aside. Whisk the yolks and the sugar together. Add the melted chocolate and about ¾ of the soaked prunes. Be sure to reserve the remaining prunes in a separate bowl for the sauce.

Lightly butter or spray with vegetable oil 2 round (8-inch) cake pans. Line the pans with parchment paper. For the larger recipe, prepare 8 pans.

For 2 cakes: Beat the egg whites until stiff and fold them gently into the chocolate mixture. Pour into the prepared pans. Bake in the center of the oven at 350 F for about 30 minutes or until springy to the touch. Allow to cool in the pan and when cold, peel off the paper, wrap well in plastic, and leave in the refrigerator for a few hours.

For 8 cakes: Beat only half of the egg whites until stiff then fold them gently into half of the chocolate mixture. Divide this mixture between 4 of the prepared pans and bake as described above. Leave the remaining batter at room temperature undisturbed until needed.

To complete the baking, beat the remaining egg whites until stiff, combine with the rest of the batter and proceed as above.

The cakes can be made 2 to 3 days in advance. Bring to room temperature for serving.

Sauce aux Pruneaux et Crème Fraîche (Armagnac Prune Cream)

Blend or purée the reserved prunes in advance, if desired, but do not add the crème fraîche until a few hours . before serving.

For 25 servings   For 100 servings

3 C (750 ml)   crème fraîche (see recipe p.151)   6 C (1 ½ l)
                     remaining soaked prunes

Using a blender, food processor, or immersion wand, blend the remaining prunes and their liquid until smooth. Place in a bowl; swirl in the crème fraîche lightly and serve separately as a sauce for the cakes.

Lemon Pudding Cake

Jim's good friend and frequent Sunday dinner cook Barbara Sherman adapted this recipe from her family's version. "My kids always loved it and I figured Jim's crowd would too." She is entirely right about that. To make the mixing easier, 3-gallon mixing bowls are ideal. This old favorite is called 'pudding cake' because when baked, the bottom becomes a creamy custard while the top is lightly crusty, something like an angel food cake. For ten cakes, be sure to allow time for two rounds of baking.

For 25 servings (3 cakes)		For 100 servings (10 cakes)
6 C (1200 g)	sugar	20 C (4 kg)
1 ½ C (190 g)	flour	5 C (625 g)
1 ¼ tsp	salt	4 tsp
3 Tb	lemon zest	10 Tb
12	eggs	40
6 C (1 ½ l)	whole milk	5 qt (5 L)
1 ½ C (6 lemons)	lemon juice	5 C (20 lemons)

Sift the sugar, flour, and salt into a large bowl. Add the zest.

Separate the eggs, setting aside the whites. Beat the eggs yolks until creamy and then, add the milk. Add the flour mixture to the egg yolk mixture, stirring to combine. Add the lemon juice.

For 3 cakes: Beat the egg whites until they are stiff then fold them gently into the flour mixture. Divide the mixture between 3 (2-quart) baking dishes (loaf pans are ideal). Place the baking dishes into larger pans. Pour hot water into the larger pans to a depth of about 1 inch. A large roasting pan may accommodate all 3 cakes. Bake at 350 F for 50 minutes.

For 10 cakes: Beat only half of the egg whites until they are stiff then fold them gently into half of the flour mixture. Leave the remaining batter at room temperature undisturbed until needed. Divide the mixture between 5 (2-quart) baking dishes and proceed as above. Bake the remaining 5 cakes using the reserved batter and remaining egg whites as described.

Cool and serve the cakes from their pans.

Pineapple Upside-Down Cake

Although everyone has heard of this classic cake in North America, many people who dine at Jim's in Paris find it exotic and curious. This does not cause them to hesitate over seconds, however. The batter is not complicated but to make the larger recipe, assemble all the ingredients and combine only enough for four cakes at one time. Continue the process three times for twelve cakes. Be sure to have enough large plates or trays to accommodate the cakes when they are turned out.

For 25 servings (4 cakes)		For 100 servings (12 cakes)
1 lb (500 g)	butter, melted	4 lb (2 kg)
2 C (500 g)	brown sugar	8 C (2 kg)
3 lb (1 ½ kg)	pineapple slices, fresh or canned	12 lb (6 kg)
2 lb (1 kg)	butter, softened	8 lb (4 kg)
8 C (1600 g)	sugar	32 C (6 kg)
16	eggs	64
12 C (1 ½ kg)	flour	12 lb (6 kg)
1 tsp	salt	4 tsp
4 Tb	double-acting baking powder	1 C (180 g)
1 qt (1 L)	milk	4 qt (4 L)

Distribute the melted butter evenly among 4 (9-inch) round cake pans, followed by the brown sugar. Arrange the sliced pineapple on the butter and sugar mixture. Use 12 pans for the larger recipe.

Cream the butter and sugar until light and fluffy in a large mixing bowl. Add the eggs. Beat until light.

Mix the flour, salt, and baking powder together. Add these dry ingredients alternately with the milk to the butter and sugar mixture. Beat well. Spread the batter over the pineapple.

For the larger recipe, make 4 cakes at one time and refrigerate the batter between baking times.

Bake in a moderate oven (325 F) about 1 hour. Cool for 5 minutes and then invert onto large plates or serving trays.

Pain d'Epice with Gingered Pears

Honey is the sweetener in pain d'épice, a French spice cake that is much like gingerbread. It can be served with whipped cream, whipped crème fraîche, warm applesauce or my favorite: gingered pears. This wonderful fall dessert calls for willing volunteers to peel pears and help with baking. Pain d'épice keeps very well and can be made in advance. Be sure to determine beforehand how many pans your oven will accommodate.

For 25 servings (2 cakes)		For 100 servings (8 cakes)
5 C (625 g)	flour	20 C (2 ½ kg)
1 tsp	baking soda	4 tsp
1 tsp	salt	4 tsp
3 Tb	fresh ginger, grated	2 (6-inch) pieces
3 Tb	crystallized ginger, finely chopped	12 oz (340 g)
1 tsp each	cinnamon, cloves, nutmeg, allspice	4 tsp each
½ tsp	ginger, ground	1 Tb
1 Tb	cocoa	4 Tb
½ lb (250 g)	butter, melted	2 lb (1 kg)
1 C (250 ml)	honey	1 qt (1 L)
1 C (200 g)	sugar	4 C (800 g)
1 C	buttermilk	1 qt (1 L)
1 C	milk	1 qt (1 L)
3	eggs	12

Grease and flour 2 (9 x 13-inch) baking pans. Prepare 8 pans for 100 servings.

Combine flour, baking soda, salt, all the ginger, cinnamon, cloves, nutmeg, allspice, and cocoa in a large bowl. In a separate bowl, beat the butter, honey, sugar, buttermilk, milk, and eggs until well combined.

Add the honey and milk mixture to the dry ingredients, beat until smooth and thick, about 1 minute. Don't over mix. For the larger recipe, make 2 cakes at a time (or 4 if your oven will accommodate the pans). Refrigerate the batter between baking times.

Pour batter in the pans and bake in a moderately hot oven (350 F) about 35 to 45 minutes.

Cool the cakes on racks for 10 minutes. Can be left in the pans until serving time.

Gingered Pears in Port

This Port-infused compote is sweetened with honey complimenting the pain d'épice. For a stronger ginger flavor, crystallized ginger can be added at serving time.

For 25 servings		For 100 servings
4 lb (2 kg)	firm pears, peeled, cored and quartered	20 lb (9 kg)
½ C (2 lemons)	lemon juice	2 C (8 lemons)
2 C	honey	2 qt (2 L)
½ C (100 g)	sugar	2 C (400 g)
2 C	Port	2 bottles
2-inch piece	ginger, peeled and cut in 2 or 3 pieces	8-inch piece
	Optional:	
3 Tb	crystallized ginger, finely chopped	12 oz (340 g)

Peel, core, and quarter the pears, putting them one or more large bowls with cold water to cover. Add a few tablespoons of the lemon juice (about ½ cup for the larger recipe) to keep the pears from browning.

In a pot large enough to hold the pears, bring the remaining lemon juice, honey, sugar, port, and ginger to a boil and simmer for about 10 minutes. Add the pears and enough water to cover. Bring to the boil, lower the heat, and simmer until pears are just softened, about 15 minutes. Turn off the heat and let cool completely. Remove the pears from the liquid to deep bowls or pans. Reduce the liquid by half until it is syrupy. Discard the ginger pieces. Cool the syrup, pour over the pears, and refrigerate until serving time.

If desired, sprinkle the pears with the crystallized ginger.

Strawberry Refrigerator Cheesecake

This easy no-bake recipe has been around in various forms since the 1970's and has stood the test of time. Fresh strawberries really make a difference here and it is worth seeking out the sweetest, ripest ones you can find.

For 25 servings		For 100 servings
4 C (375 g)	cookie crumbs or graham crackers	3 lb (1 ½ kg)
1 C (200 g)	brown sugar	1 ½ lb (750 g)
6 oz (200 g)	butter, melted	1 ½ lb (750 g)
4–5	lemons	16–20
2 lb (900 g)	cream cheese, softened	6 lb (2 ½ kg)
4 cans	sweetened condensed milk (14 oz or 397 g)	12 cans
4 tsp	vanilla	4 Tbs
4 lb (2 kg)	strawberries, sliced or quartered	12 lb (5 kg)
1 C (200 g)	sugar, approximately	3–4 C (700 g)

For the crumb crust, mix the crumbs, brown sugar, and butter together. Press into 1 (12 x 16-inch) or 2 (9 x 13-inch) baking pans. For 100 servings, use 4 large pans. Cook 5 minutes in a moderate oven (325 F) and cool completely.

Squeeze the lemons. You will need 1 cup of juice (3 cups for the larger recipe). In a large bowl, combine the cream cheese, condensed sweetened milk, lemon juice, and vanilla. Beat several minutes until smooth and creamy. Pour into the prepared crusts and refrigerate several hours.

Mix the strawberries with enough sugar to lightly sweeten them and let stand at room temperature for about 30 minutes. Spread the strawberries over the chilled cheesecakes. You may also serve the berries separately, spooning some over each cheesecake serving.

Pine Nut Cookies

These are elegant little cookies: crisp, buttery, and not too sweet. This recipe serves about three average size cookies per person. Using parchment or baking paper is highly recommended, as the cookies are fragile when hot. Quickly lifting the entire sheet off the baking tray eliminates using a spatula to transfer each cookie. Serve these with fresh fruit. In summer, a good choice would be fresh cherries, sliced watermelon, or a melon salad.

For 25 servings (7 dozen)		For 100 servings (28 dozen)
½ lb +2 Tb (275 g)	butter, softened	2 ½ lb (1100 g)
1 ¼ C (150 g)	powdered sugar	5 C (600 g)
4 Tb	sugar	1 C (200 g)
1 tsp	vanilla	4 tsp
1 ½ C (185 g)	flour	6 C (740 g)
1 tsp	salt	4 tsp
½ tsp (scant)	baking powder	1 ½ tsp
6 oz (180 g)	pine nuts	1 ½ lb (720 g)

Beat together the butter and sugars. Add vanilla. In a separate bowl, mix the flour, salt, and baking powder.

Toast the pine nuts lightly in a dry frying pan either over medium heat or in the microwave. Watch very carefully as they burn easily. Let cool. Grind half the pine nuts in a food processor or blender.

Add flour mixture and all the nuts to the butter and sugar mixture. Drop by rounded teaspoons, 2 inches apart (these cookies spread) onto baking sheets lined with parchment paper. Bake in a moderately hot oven (325 F) 8 to 10 minutes or until set and brown on the edges. Carefully transfer to racks to cool completely. Lifting or sliding the entire sheet of parchment onto a rack or the counter is a good way to handle this process.

This cookie dough may be made in advance and refrigerated a few days or frozen. Once baked, the cookies will keep very well in tightly sealed bags or boxes for 2 weeks.

Brownies

Along with bagels, 'les broonies' are a huge American hit in Paris and this very rich, chewy version is pounced on at Jim's parties. They can be made well in advance. Serve with strawberries or cut up watermelon for an easy summer dessert.

For 25 servings (about 30 squares)		For 100 servings (about 120 squares)
1 ¾ lb (750 g)	semi-sweet or bittersweet chocolate	7 lb (3 kg)
1 ¾ lb (750 g)	butter	7 lb (3 kg)
1 Tb	vanilla	3 Tb
1 dozen	eggs, slightly beaten	4 dozen
4 C (800 g)	sugar	16 C (3 ¼ kg)
3 C (375 g)	flour	12 C (1 ½ kg)
¾ tsp	salt	1 Tb
	Optional:	
1 lb (500 g)	chopped nuts	4 lb (2 kg)

Melt the chocolate with the butter in a bain-marie or in a microwave oven. Do this in batches as necessary. Cool slightly and add vanilla and eggs. Combine the sugar and flour and add to the chocolate mixture, stirring until just combined. Add chopped nuts if desired. Pour into 1 large (12 by 16 inch) buttered pan. For 100 servings, use 4 large pans and bake 2 at a time. Refrigerate the batter between bakings. Bake for 30 minutes in a moderately hot oven (350 F) or until just cooked through. Cool and cut into squares.

Seven Layer Bars

One word: easy. Starting with the store-bought cookies, this is basically an exercise in layering. For Jim's dinners in Paris, these bars are made with "Petit Beurres" but any dry cookie will do. These very sweet, almost candy-like bars can be made in advance and keep very well. A small square suffices but generally, people come back for more.

For 25 servings		For 100 servings
8 oz (250 g)	butter, melted	2 lb (1 kg)
2 C (200 g)	cookie crumbs or graham crackers	8 C (800 g)
12 oz (375 g)	semi-sweet chocolate chips or bars, broken in pieces	3 lb (1 ½ kg)
8 oz (250 g)	nuts, chopped	2 lb (1 kg)
6 oz (200 g)	grated coconut	1 ½ lb (800 g)
1 C (125 g)	raisins	1 lb (500 g)
2 ½ C (600 ml)	sweetened condensed milk	10 C (2 ½ L)

Distribute the melted butter evenly in 2 (9 x 13-inch) baking pans. For 100 servings, use 8 pans. Top with the cookie crumbs, then the chocolate, then the nuts, the coconut, and the raisins, distributing each ingredient evenly between the pans. Pour on the sweetened condensed milk last. Bake in a moderately hot oven (350 F) for about 30 minutes or until golden brown. For the larger recipe, bake 2 pans at a time (or 4 if your oven space permits). Cool and cut into small squares, as this is a very rich, sweet dessert.

Sharp Lemon Tart

A rich and tangy dessert. Grating and squeezing the lemons takes some time but there is no substitute for fresh lemons. A slightly sweet crust made with ground almonds compliments the lemon filling. Both the filling and the crust may be made a day ahead. Although this is a tart, there is almost a quart of filling per pie so do not use pans that are too shallow.

For 25 servings

Crust:

		For 100 servings
¾ C (100 g)	almonds, finely ground	3 C (450 g)
6 ¾ C	flour	27 C
¼ tsp	salt	1 tsp
12 oz (350 g)	unsalted butter	3 lb
2 ¼ C (280 g)	powdered sugar, sifted	9 C (1 ¼ kg)
3	eggs, lightly beaten	12
¼ tsp	vanilla or lemon extract	1 tsp

Crust:

Sift the ground almonds, flour, and salt together. Work the butter into the sugar quickly and add to the flour mixture. Mix in the beaten eggs with the extract. Chill for a couple of hours. Using a food processor will facilitate this process.

The dough can be rolled, but tends to be sticky so roll it between sheets of waxed paper or simply, press it evenly into the pan. Do not roll it too thinly. Use 1 (12 x 16-inch) pan for 25 servings (or 4 pans for the larger recipe.)

Line the tart shell(s) with aluminum foil, pressing the foil firmly onto the crust. Prick with a fork through the foil. Bake for 10 minutes at 425 F. Remove the foil and bake for 5 minutes more. Let cool.

Lemon filling:

12	lemons	48
27	eggs	9 dozen
4 ½ C (900 g)	sugar	18 C (3 ½ kg)
4 ½ C (1 ¼ L)	heavy cream	4 ½ qt (4 ½ L)
	whipped cream (see recipe p.151)	

Grate the zest from all the lemons and squeeze the juice. Beat the eggs until well mixed; add lemon juice, zest, and sugar. Beat cream separately until slightly thick and add to mixture.

Place the tart shell(s) in the oven set to 300 F. To avoid spilling, use a pitcher to pour in the lemon mixture. Bake until set and the tart feels firm and springy to the touch, about 1 hour and 15 minutes. Check after 50 minutes.

Allow the tarts to cool for at least ½ hour and serve small pieces with whipped cream, if desired.

Pecan Pie

At Thanksgiving, nostalgic Americans flock to Jim Haynes for a traditional feast that includes pecan pie. Catherine Monnet recalls, "For years, we had to count on American visitors importing the pecans and corn syrup in their suitcases." Now readily available in Paris, these imported ingredients are still expensive. This is an easy pie to make and about as sweet as they come. One pie will serve eight to ten people. Can be prepared a day or two in advance.

For 25 servings (3 pies)		For 100 servings (12 pies)
3	ready-to-bake tart shells	12
6 Tb	butter, melted	1 ½ lb (750 g)
2 C (500 g)	sugar (use brown, white or a mixture)	8 C (1600 g)
9	eggs, well-beaten	36
1 ½ bottles	dark Karo corn syrup (16 oz)	6 bottles
1 ½ tsp	salt	2 Tb
1 Tb	vanilla	4 Tb
6 C (600 g)	whole pecans	24 C (2 ½ kg)

Mix together butter, sugar, eggs, corn syrup, salt, and vanilla.

Spread 2 cups of pecans on the bottom of each pie shell. Pour on the filling, distributing evenly. For 10 pies, bake 3 or 4 pies at a time, pouring the filling just before baking so that the crusts do not become soggy.

Bake in a moderately hot oven (350 F) for about 45 minutes.

FRUIT AND PUDDINGS

Homemade Applesauce

Use a mix of apples and just a suggestion of sugar. Using a food mill means no peeling or coring apples. You can also press the purée through a large strainer or colander with the back of a wooden spoon. This is a simple dessert, good with a cookie on the side or as a side dish with ham or roast pork.

For 25 servings		For 100 servings
6 lb (2 ½ kg)	mixed unpeeled apples, tart and sweet, quartered	22 lb (10 kg)
2 tsp	cinnamon	2 Tb
1 tsp	nutmeg	1 Tb
3 Tb	sugar (or to taste)	1 C (200 g)

Pour about ½ inch water in the bottom of a large stockpot, add all the apples, cover, and bring to a boil under medium high heat. Lower the heat and cook, stirring from time to time until the apples are completely soft and lose their shape. Add more water if necessary to keep from sticking.

Purée the apples in batches using a food mill into a large bowl. While still warm, stir in the cinnamon, nutmeg, and a minimum of sugar. Taste and add more sugar and spices, if desired. Let cool and refrigerate. For serving, allow the purée to come to room temperature.

Cherry Clafoutis

Somewhere between custard and a pudding, clafoutis is a beloved French dessert traditionally made with unpitted sour cherries. So as not to risk broken teeth with unsuspecting guests, this recipe omits the pits but adds ground almonds to evoke the original taste. If you are lucky enough to have a source of fresh cherries, gather some volunteers and go to town pitting. Otherwise, frozen cherries will do nicely.

For 25 servings		For 100 servings
	butter for pans	
4 lb (2 kg)	cherries, *fresh or frozen, well drained	16 lb (8 kg)
1 ¼ C (250 g)	sugar	5 C (1 kg)
1 ¼ C (160 g)	flour	5 C (625 g)
¾ C (100 g)	ground almonds	3 C (450 g)
12	eggs	48
3 C (750 ml)	whole milk	3 qt (3 L)
6 oz (190 g)	butter, melted	1 ½ lb (750 g)
2 tsp	vanilla	3 Tb
	Optional:	
4 Tb	powdered sugar	1 C (125 g)

Butter 1 large (12 x 16-inch) or 2 (9 x 13-inch) pans. Use 4 large or 8 smaller pans for 100 servings. Distribute the cherries among the pans.

Mix the sugar, flour, and ground almonds. Beat the eggs with the milk, butter, and vanilla. Gradually add the flour mixture to the egg mixture and beat until smooth. Pour the batter evenly over the cherries. Bake in a moderate oven (325 F) for 40 to 50 minutes or until lightly puffed and cooked through. Serve warm or at room temperature.

*If your cherries are sweet, reduce the sugar by half.

Chocolate Bread Pudding

Chocolate desserts are very appealing in winter although Jim Haynes, a self-confessed chocoholic, will eat chocolate any time. Leftover baguette from the Sunday dinners was the incentive for this dessert. Sprinkling the surface of the pudding with some additional sugar will add a crunchy texture or you may serve it with whipped cream. Either way will surely satisfy the sugar and chocolate lovers!

For 25 servings		For 100 servings
	butter for pans	
3 (about 16 C)	day-old baguettes, cubed	10 (about 40 C)
3 qt (3 L)	whole milk or half and half	12 qt (12 L)
2 C (200 g)	sugar	8 C (800 g)
½ tsp	salt	2 tsp
2 ½ lb (1 kg)	bittersweet chocolate, chopped	10 lb (4 kg)
2 dozen	eggs	8 dozen
1 Tb	vanilla	4 Tb
	Optional:	
½ C (100 g)	sugar	2 C (400 g)
	whipped cream (see recipe p.151)	

Butter 1 large (12 x 16-inch) or 2 (9 x 13-inch) pans. Use 4 large or 8 smaller pans for 100 servings. Distribute the bread cubes between the pans.

Bring the milk, sugar, and salt to a simmer in a large pot, stirring until the sugar dissolves. Remove from heat. Add the chocolate to the hot milk mixture and whisk until melted and smooth.

Whisk eggs and vanilla in large bowl to blend. Gradually add the hot chocolate mixture to the eggs, stirring continuously. Pour this custard over each prepared pan and leave the pans undisturbed for about an hour to allow the custard to soak into the bread.

Sprinkle the pans with the additional sugar, if desired, and bake in a moderate oven (325 F) until the custard thickens, the pudding puffs slightly and the center is just set, about 50 minutes. Do not over bake as the pudding will continue to cook as it cools.

Serve warm or at room temperature. A dollop of whipped cream may be added at serving time. The pudding can be made in advance and reheated or served at room temperature.

Fruit Crumble

Crumble is a great make-ahead dessert for a crowd. The following recipe is a super all-purpose formula for fruits of all seasons. Mixtures of fruits such as apples and plums or pears and apricots make especially good crumbles. Hazelnuts, almonds, or pecans add to the flavor and texture.

For 25 servings   For 100 servings

Fruit mixture

	butter	
8 lb (4 kg)	choice of: pears, apples, peaches, plums, apricots, or a mixture	32 lb (14 kg)
½ C (2 lemons)	lemon juice	2 C (8 lemons)
1 C (200 g)	sugar or less	4 C (800 g)
2 tsp	cinnamon	3 Tb
½ tsp	nutmeg	2 tsp

Topping

2 ½ C (300 g)	flour	10 C (1 ¼ kg)
2 ½ C (250 g)	oatmeal	10 C (1 kg)
1 ¾ C (375 g)	brown sugar	7 C (1 ½ kg)
2 tsp	cinnamon	2 ½ Tb
1 ½ tsp	salt	2 Tb
1 lb (500 g)	butter	4 lb (2 kg)
	Optional:	
2 C (300 g)	nuts, chopped or slivered	2 ½ lb (1 kg)

Butter 1 large (12 x 16-inch) or 2 (9 x 13-inch) pans. Use 4 large or 8 smaller pans for 100 servings.

Prepare the fruit by peeling, coring, and slicing as necessary. If your fruit is very sweet and ripe, reduce the amount of sugar by a third. Mix the sugar, cinnamon, and nutmeg together and toss with the fruit and lemon juice. Distribute evenly among the pans.

For the topping, combine the flour, oatmeal, sugar, cinnamon, and salt. Cut the butter in small pieces and work in lightly. You want the topping to be crumbly not oily. Add nuts, if desired. Distribute the topping over the fruit. Bake in a moderately hot oven (350 F) for 45 minutes to 1 hour.

For the larger recipe, bake this dessert in two or more rounds, leaving the prepared pans at room temperature between bakings.

Can be prepared in advance and served with cream or ice cream.

Gajer Halwa (Carrot Pudding)

This sweet, slight gooey dessert is hard to resist. It is particularly delicious following a spicy meal. Antonia Hoogewerf was given this recipe by the chef at a Punjabi wedding in Delhi where the pudding was decorated with edible silver leaves. A food processor is a huge help for grating what will look like a mountain of carrots. Lacking that, assemble some volunteers.

For 25 servings		For 100 servings
3 lb (1 ¼ kg)	carrots	12 lb (5 kg)
1 ½ qt (1 ½ L)	whole milk	6 qt (6 L)
15	cardamom pods	50
3 tsp	ground cardamom	10 tsp
3 C (600 g)	sugar	12 C (2 ½ kg)
10 oz (300 g)	butter, melted	2 ½ lb (1 ¼ kg)
½ C (125 ml)	olive oil	2 C (500 ml)
2 C (300 g)	golden raisins	2 ½ lb (1 ¼ kg)
10 oz (300 g)	pistachio nuts	2 ½ lb (1 ¼ kg)
	Optional:	
1 ½ qt (1 ½ L)	heavy cream	6 qt (6 L)

Peel the carrots and grate them. Heat the milk in a heavy pan and stir in the cardamom pods and powder. Add the grated carrots. Bring to the boil, reduce heat to medium, and cook uncovered until all liquid has been absorbed. This could take well over an hour for the large quantity.

Heat the oil and melted butter in another pan and add to the carrot mixture. Stir well and fry until carrots become red, about 30 minutes.

Add the sugar, raisins, and chopped pistachio nuts and stir thoroughly. Turn the mixture into 1 or 2 (9 x 13-inch or larger) baking pans for serving. For the larger recipe, use four pans or more, as needed.

Can be made in advance. Using shallow bowls, serve spoonfuls of the pudding warm or at room temperature with heavy cream.

Melon salad with honey, mint and ginger

A fresh fruit dessert is always appreciated, especially in the summer. Look for ripe fragrant melons and cut them the afternoon of your party for maximum flavor. Just how much melon you need depends a lot on the type and size of melon you choose. You need close to a pound of watermelon per person but less than that for cantaloupe. The weight amount listed in this recipe is a guide; you should count out enough melons for your crowd. For example, twenty-five small cantaloupes cut in quarters will provide one hundred servings. To preserve the freshest, juiciest taste in this very simple dessert, cut the melon in large slices rather than small cubes.

For 25 servings		For 100 servings
20 lb (9 kg)	assorted melons (cantaloupe, honeydew, watermelon)	80 lb (35 kg)
2-inch piece	ginger, peeled	8-inch piece
3	limes	10
1 lb (500 g)	honey	4 lb (2 kg)
¾ C (187 ml)	white wine	3 C (565 ml)
1 bunch	mint, leaves only	3 bunches

Wash all melon before cutting. Cut a small slice off the top and bottom of each melon and rest it on a chopping board for stability. Using a sharp knife, cut away the peel in strips, working from top to bottom. For cantaloupe and honeydew, cut lengthwise, remove the seeds and pith, and cut into quarters or eighths depending on the size of the melon. For watermelon, cut into quarters, then into thick slices. Cover and refrigerate the melon.

Cut the peeled ginger into slices. Squeeze the limes. Put the juice into a large saucepan along with the honey, wine, ginger, and about 1/3 of the mint leaves. Bring to a boil stirring occasionally. Simmer about 5 minutes. Set aside for several hours.

Strain the honey syrup. Serve 1 or 2 slices of melon (depending on the size) in a small bowl. Pour on a few spoonfuls of the syrup and garnish with mint.

Orange Salad with Saffron Yogurt

A deliciously refreshing dessert but it is labor intensive, so you should have a few willing peelers and slicers around. Best made the day before and served cold so that the cardamom syrup really flavors the oranges. The saffron yogurt is optional and is good by itself.

For 25 servings		For 100 servings
25	large oranges	100
2 C (500 ml)	water	2 qt (2 L)
4 Tb	brown sugar	1 C (200 g)
4 Tb	sugar	1 C (200 g)
1 ½ tsp	vanilla	2 Tb
5	cardamom pods	20
1 ½ tsp	ground cardamom	2 Tb
2 ½ tsp	cinnamon	10 tsp
1 ½ tsp	cumin seeds, optional	2 Tb

Make a syrup by boiling the water with sugar, vanilla, cardamom pods, ground cardamom, and cinnamon, adding the cumin seeds if desired. Watch and stir frequently to avoid boiling over. Reduce by about half or until thickened.

Peel and slice oranges and place in a large bowl. Pour warm syrup over oranges and allow to cool completely. Refrigerate several hours or overnight before serving. Serve with saffron yogurt.

Saffron Yogurt

2 Tb	milk	6 Tb
1 tsp	saffron strands	1 Tb
3 C (750 ml)	plain yogurt	3 qt (3 L)
4 Tb	sugar	1 C (200 g)

Warm the milk briefly in the microwave oven. Soak the saffron strands in the milk until softened, about 10 minutes. Add this mixture to the yogurt, together with the sugar.

Southern Banana Trifle

Trifle conjures up the English dessert but at Jim's Sunday dinner, a guest from Louisiana said it tasted just like her mother's Southern banana pudding. It consists of layers of cake, jam, custard sauce, bananas and whipped cream. The custard sauce is the only part of the recipe that takes some time and concentration. Otherwise, this is a lot of fun to put together and scrumptious to eat. Make a day ahead.

For 25 servings		For 100 servings
12	eggs, yolks only	48
1 C (200 g)	sugar	4 C (800 g)
1 C (125 g)	flour	4 C (500 g)
1 qt (1 L)	milk	4 qt (4 L)
2 Tb	vanilla	8 Tb
2 ½ lb (1 kg)	store-bought pound cake, sliced thin	9 lb (4 kg)
½ C (125 ml)	orange juice	2 C (500 ml)
½ C (125 ml)	rum	2 C (500 ml)
8 oz (250 g)	strawberry jam	2 lb (1 kg)
4 lb (1 ¾ kg)	bananas, peeled and sliced	16 lb (7 kg)
1 qt (1 L)	crème fraîche (see recipe p. 151) or cream	4 qt (4 L)
1 C (125 g)	powdered or superfine sugar	4 C (500 g)
1 C (150 g)	almonds, sliced, toasted	1 lb (500 g)

In a large bowl, beat the egg yolks with the sugar until they are very thick and pale yellow. Add the flour and beat well. Heat the milk until hot but not boiling and gradually, add it to the egg mixture, stirring constantly.

Transfer the mixture to a large pot and cook, stirring constantly with a whisk, until it is thick and starts to boil. Add the vanilla and let cool.

Combine the orange juice and rum. Using a pastry brush, lightly moisten the cake slices with this mixture. Line the bottom of 1-inch deep (14 by 16 inch) baking pan with half the cake slices. Use 4 pans for 100 servings.

Mix the jam with any of the leftover juice mixture and brush over the cake slices. Pour half the custard sauce over the jam-topped cake slices. Evenly distribute the sliced bananas on top of the custard and then top with the rest of the custard, pushing the bananas in to cover completely (so they will not turn brown).

Top the banana cream layer with the other half of the cake slices, creating a sort of sandwich.

Whip the cream with the powdered sugar. Cover the cake slices with the whipped cream and sprinkle with the toasted almonds. Chill the trays of banana trifle in the refrigerator at least 6 hours or overnight. Scoop out with a spatula to serve.

Strawberries in Balsamic Vinegar

Preparing this Italian springtime dessert is as simple as it gets, particularly if there are helpers with the strawberries. The vinegar adds a surprising velvety taste that few can identify at first. In Paris, it is possible to find tiny "fraises des bois" starting in mid-April. They are very tender and sweet, much like an Oregon strawberry, and are perfect for this dessert. Try to find the juiciest, freshest berries in your area.

For 25 servings		For 100 servings
7 lb (3 kg)	strawberries	27 lb (12 kg)
1 C (200 g)	sugar	4 C (800 g)
1 C (250 ml)	balsamic vinegar	1 qt (1 L)

Wipe or quickly rinse the strawberries, remove the stems, and quarter them. If the berries are small, leave them whole. About 2 hours before serving, combine the berries with just enough sugar to sweeten them in 1 or more large bowls. Add the balsamic vinegar and mix gently to coat. Stir occasionally.

Serve in small bowls.

Pineapple Sundae with Caramel Sauce and Ice Cream

On a warm June evening in Paris, Jim Haynes's guests raved about this fresh pineapple sundae.
The caramel sauce can be the starting point for all kinds of ice cream desserts or served with cake or bread
puddings. It can be made days in advance and even frozen for longer storage.

For 25 servings		For 100 servings
1 lb (500 g)	sugar	4 lb (2 kg)
1 lb (500 g)	butter	4 lb (2 kg)
1 C (250 ml)	crème fraîche (see recipe p.151)	1 qt (1 L)
	or heavy cream	
1 tsp	salt*	1 heaping Tb
4	pineapples	16
3 qt (3 L)	vanilla ice cream	10 qt (10 L)

In a large pot over low heat, melt the sugar without stirring until it bubbles around the edges. Add the butter, cut in pieces but do not stir. When the butter starts to melt, stir gently until the mixture is a homogenous mass. Cool a few minutes and add the cream and salt. Serve warm or cold.

Peel the pineapples, remove the tough inner core, and cut into cubes. Cover and refrigerate until serving time.

To serve, top a scoop of vanilla ice cream with a spoonful of pineapple and some of the caramel sauce.

*Kosher salt, sea salt or fleur de sel are recommended.

Crème Fraîche I

Many of the recipes in this book call for crème fraîche, which is a slightly sour, thick cream sold commonly in France. Unlike sour cream, it will not curdle if boiled and can be whipped. Crème fraîche can be found in the United States but is expensive. Here is a method for making a large quantity of crème fraîche that is very close to the real thing.

2 qt (2 L)	heavy cream, *not* ultra-pasteurized
1 C (250 ml)	buttermilk

Combine the cream and buttermilk in a large glass baking pan or bowl. Cover and let stand at room temperature from 8 to 24 hours, or until very thick. Stir well and store in a covered container. Crème fraîche will keep well refrigerated for up to 10 days.

Crème Fraîche II

This super-quick version will not thicken but will approximate the tangy flavor of crème fraîche.

2 qt (2 L)	heavy cream
5 C (1 ¼ L)	sour cream

Stir the two creams together thoroughly and refrigerate, covered.

Whipped Cream

When figuring out how much whipped cream to make as an accompaniment for desserts, count on two tablespoons of heavy cream per person.

For 25 servings		For 100 servings
2 C (500 ml)	heavy cream	2 qt (2 L)
2 Tb	sugar	8 Tb
1 Tb	vanilla	4 Tb

Chill the cream, bowl, and beaters. Beat until soft peaks form; add the sugar, and continue to beat until stiff peaks form.

COCKTAILS and PUNCH

Hug and kiss every chance you get. To encourage anyone to be more loving is, surely, something well worth doing.

Jim Haynes

Helen's Wedding Punch

When asked the secret of a successful party, a veteran hostess promptly responded, "Serve alcohol." Few would disagree, nevertheless, providing an alternative is important. Helen Cohen, of Washington DC, came up with this punch for a wedding. It is non-alcoholic, refreshing, and not too sweet.

For 2 gallons 64 (4-ounce) servings		For 4 gallons 128 (4-ounce) servings
2 qt (2 L)	cranberry juice	4 qt (4 L)
2 qt (2 L)	grapefruit juice	4 qt (4 L)
2 qt (2 L)	guava-passion fruit juice	4 qt (4 L)
4	limes, cut in slices or quarters	8
2 qt (2 L)	ginger ale or sparkling water	4 qt (4 L)

Mix the juices. Just before serving, add ginger ale and float lime slices. For an even less sweet punch, use sparkling water instead of ginger ale or some of each.

Fresh Fruity Sherbet Punch

Care to time travel? At parties circa 1950, the floating sherbet punch was de rigueur! Using a large block of ice will keep this one cold for a long time.

Makes about 40 servings

2 C (500 ml) orange juice, freshly squeezed
2 C (500 ml) lime juice, freshly squeezed
2 C (500 ml) pineapple juice
1 qt (1 L) orange sherbet
2 qt (2 L) ginger ale
1 bunch mint
4 oranges, sliced

Mix the juices and add the sherbet by spoonfuls. Pour over a large block of ice in a large punch bowl. Just before serving, add the ginger ale and garnish with mint leaves and orange slices.

Vodka Mojitos

At his annual bash for Insta-Fame Studios in Portland, Oregon, producer Ben Lund makes dynamite mojitos. He mixes up a big batch of the mojito base in advance, puts it in gallon milk jugs and stores it on ice. Add plenty of sparkling water and ice to each drink. This will make approximately 100 drinks.

3 bunches mint, leaves only
6 C lime juice
4 C (800 g) sugar
6 bottles vodka
8 liters club soda or sparkling water

Using a wooden spoon, mash the mint leaves with lime juice and sugar until well combined and the sugar dissolves. Add the vodka and chill several hours. Serve with ice and club soda or sparkling water.

Pomegranate Martinis

A detour on the road to the Cosmopolitan. Pomegranate juice, tart enough to stand up to the Cointreau, makes this a delicious and powerful drink.

Makes 25 cocktails

1 (750 ml) bottle vodka
12 oz (325 ml) Cointreau
2 ¼ qt (2 ¼ L) pomegranate juice
Garnish: lemon wedges

Combine the ingredients and chill. Serve with ice in a small glass with a lemon wedge. You can also pour 1 or 2 drinks at a time in a shaker with crushed ice and serve in martini glasses.

Sangria

There are endless variations to Sangria. This basic recipe makes about 3 ½ gallons or about 100 (4-ounce) servings.

10 (750 ml) bottles light red wine
1 bottle brandy
1 bottle triple sec or Grand Marnier
10 oranges, sliced
5 lemons, sliced
5 limes, sliced
5 liter bottles club soda or sparkling water

Mix all ingredients and let sit for 2 hours. Serve over ice.

White Sangria

Ripe peaches and nectarines make this white sangria a very pleasant, summer drink. This version calls for orgeat syrup, which is made of almonds and a small amount of orange flower water. Almond syrup can be found at specialty stores and is sometimes used to flavor coffee.

For 100 drinks or 3 ½ gallons

24 ripe peaches or nectarines
12 (750 ml) bottles Cava, Prosecco or sparkling white wine
2 (750 ml) bottles orgeat or almond syrup
45 liter bottles club soda or sparkling water

Slice the fruit thinly and mix with 2 bottles of the sparkling wine. Refrigerate for 2 hours or over-night. Chill the sparkling wine and water. To serve, mix the fruit and wine base with the remaining wine, 1 ½ bottles of the almond syrup, and 4 liters of sparkling water. Add more syrup and sparkling water to taste.

To preserve the fizz in the sangria, you may also mix it in smaller batches using only a portion of the fruit base and adding 1 or 2 bottles of sparkling wine at a time and the syrup to taste.

Serve from pitchers.

Coffee Punch

This punch can be served as a dessert with a tray of cookies and fruit. Sweet and cold, it makes a refreshing alternative to hot coffee, especially in the summer.

For 50 servings

1 gallon (4 L) coffee (French roast or espresso roast)
1 qt (1 L) heavy cream
5 Tb sugar
5 tsp vanilla
1 qt (1 L) vanilla ice cream

Brew the coffee and chill it. Whip the cream until stiff, adding the sugar and vanilla at the soft peak stage. Shortly before serving, break up the ice cream into small slices. Place the whipped cream and the ice cream in a big bowl and add the coffee. Mix well.

Moroccan Mint Tea

This is usually served hot and quite sweet. Adjust the sugar as you wish. You can also cool the tea and serve it chilled with additional fresh mint as a garnish.

For 25 servings

20 bags or 12 Tb green tea
8 qt (8 L) water
4 bunches spearmint, leaves only
4 C (800 g) sugar

Bring the water to a boil and add the tea. Let steep for a few minutes, add the mint leaves and continue to steep for several minutes. Add the sugar and stir well. Serve hot or cold, strained.

To keep tea hot for several hours, pour it into thermos bottles and seal tightly.

WHAT A GREAT PARTY

When the histories of Paris in the late twentieth and early twenty-first centuries are written, Jim Haynes and his marvelous dinners are going to be remembered for being at the vital center of a thrilling social scene.

Jake Lamar, author

The last guests leave and the outside lights are turned off. Charlie, the neighbor's cat, snoops around the garden hoping to find a few tidbits. Houseguests put away extra chairs, stack the dishes, and Jim Haynes has a look at his list. Who came to his Paris dinner that night? How many women and how many men? Who made a new friend or ran into an old one? How many languages were spoken?

Each Sunday dinner has its own energy and character but Jim Haynes is already looking ahead. He knows there are twenty or thirty people on the list for next Sunday and that the list will fill as the week goes on. His upstairs neighbor, Madame Paupèrt, knows that she will be receiving leftovers the following morning. The volunteers who cook for Jim know they will receive a call from Jim with his thanks and an invitation to lunch. In hotels and apartments all over Paris, people who have been to the dinner are thinking about their evening. Many will return to their own homes in various parts of the world and talk about Jim, the American in Paris, who throws a great party every Sunday night.

The dinners are an important part of Jim's life but so is the theater, travel, books and above all, his enormous circle of friends. On Sunday nights, you will find him at home but the rest of the week? Houseguests arrive and depart. Letters are answered (not an easy task given the volume of correspondence) and interviews are conducted. A steady stream of writers, photographers, filmmakers, students, and artists show up to visit, have a cup of tea and talk about their work. He goes out nearly every night to plays, readings, restaurants, and naturally, other people's parties.

Jim Haynes has been our muse in writing this book and we hope he will be yours as you plan your own parties. Should you find yourself in Paris, give Jim a call, and discover first-hand what throwing a great party is all about.

APPENDIX

SERVING SIZES

Food Serving Sizes

When following the recipes in this book, you will find that the amounts for 25 servings versus 100 servings are not in an exact 1 to 4 ratio. We have found that with many recipes, ingredients simply cannot be expanded or reduced automatically. The serving sizes that follow are based on broad guidelines. Consider how many servings you think your guests will eat and how you plan to serve the meal. Guests tend to eat more at a self-serve buffet so you might add an extra vegetable or salad to the menu to be sure your guests are well-fed.

	25 servings	100 servings
Soup 1 C (or 250 ml) per serving	7 qt (L)	25 qt (L)
Main Dish 5 oz (140 g) per serving	8 lb (4 kg)	32 lb (14 kg)
Vegetables 3 oz (100 g) per serving	6 lb (2 ½ kg)	22 lb (10 kg)
Salad greens 2 oz (60 g) per serving	3 lb (1 ½ kg)	13 lb (6 kg)

BAR SETUP

Your local wine and liquor purveyor should be a great resource. You will get good advice about how much and what to buy, as well as what is a good value for your money. Be prepared to discuss your budget, the weather, the size and make up of your crowd, and what kind of drinks you envision. The wine merchant will help you make your selection. Here are some general guidelines to buying alcohol.

Quantities
For a party, the standard quantity to provide is 4 drinks per person.

1 bottle wine or Champagne (750 ml) = 5 drinks
1 keg beer = 15 ½ gallons = about 150 (12 ounce) beers
1 bottle spirits (Vodka, rum, etc.) (750 ml) = 17 drinks

Ice: allow 1 pound per person.

The "Full Bar"
Just as cocktails have made a resurgence so has the fully stocked bar. If you would like to offer a "full bar" in addition to wine and beer, you will need a variety of spirits. Since it is hard to predict who will have a mixed drink, you should anticipate the added cost and some leftover liquor. The same is true of the mixers, such as tonic water and club soda. Vodka is very popular, gin less so, followed by scotch and bourbon. If it's hot out, you might add a bottle of rum or tequila.

For 25 to 30 guests: buy 2 bottles of vodka and one each of the others.

For 100 guests: 4 bottles of vodka, 2 gin, 1 scotch, 1 bourbon and 1 rum or tequila.

Here is a sample list to illustrate what you might serve 25 guests
In this case, you would be serving one special cocktail only in addition to your wine and beer.

Cocktail or mixed drink	1 to 2 bottles spirits
	4 bottles mixer, juice, etc.
	5 cut limes, lemons, or oranges
Beer	1 case, assorted
Wine (with dinner)	1 case, white, red, or mixed

Here is a sample list to illustrate what you might serve 100 guests

Sangria: 3 gallons	100 drinks
Beer: 1 keg	150 drinks
Non-alcoholic punch: 3 gallons	100 drinks
Wine: 10 bottles	50 drinks

EQUIPMENT

The following list gives some standard and large pan sizes for quantity cooking. It is very important to determine how many pans will fit in the oven space. Using the largest pans that will fit your oven is generally the most effective approach but do not overfill pans simply to save time.

	Dimensions	Volume	Portions
Baking sheets (also known as half-sheets or jellyroll)			
Standard	12 x 18 x 1 inch	10 C	4–6 dozen squares
Baking pans			
Standard	9 by 13 x 2 inch	14 C	2–3 dozen squares
Large:	13 x 18 x 2 inch	28 C	4–6 dozen squares
Roasting pans			
Standard	12 x 16 x 2 inch	20 C	
Large	12 x 20 x 2 ½ inch	30 C	
Stockpots			
Standard		12 qt	30 (1 cup)
		16 qt	50 (1 cup)
Extra-large		20 qt	70 (1 cup)
		32 qt	120 (1 cup)
		40 qt	150 (1 cup)
Pans, frying, or sauté			
Standard	10 and 12 inch		
Large	14 inch		
Bowls			
Standard		4 qt	
Large		12 qt	
		16 qt	

ADDITIONAL EQUIPMENT

The following items, not always found in home kitchens, are very helpful when dealing with large quantities.

Box grater
Chopping boards, large, heavy plastic (24 x 24 inch)
Colander, 5 quarts or larger
Heavy-duty oven mitts
Japanese vegetable slicer
Ladles, long-handled
Microplane grater
Peelers, 'Y-shaped' plastic (easy to work with)
Spoons, extra-long metal
Tongs, long and short
Whisks, large

The following small appliances are also very useful:

Blender
Immersion blender/mixer
Food processor
Microwave oven

EQUIVALENTS and MEASURES

	Weight oz/g	Volume	Other Equivalents
Baking			
Baking powder	1 oz/28g	2 ½ Tb	
Gelatin	¼ oz/7 g	1 Tb	1 envelope
Chocolate	7 oz/200 g	7 squares	1 bar
Chocolate chips	12 oz/340 g	2 C	
Sugar	8 oz/200 g	1 C	
Sugar, brown	1 lb/500g	2 ¼ C packed	
Sugar, powdered	4 oz/125 g	1 C	
Honey	11 oz/300 g	1 C	
Flour	4 oz/125 g	1 C	
	1 lb/500 g	4 C	
Oatmeal	3 ½ oz/100 g	1 C	
Cornmeal	5 ½ oz/150 g	1 C	
	1 lb/500 g	3 C	
Salt, coarse or Kosher	1 oz/28 g	2 Tb	
Salt, table	1 oz/28 g	1 ½ Tb	
Pepper	1 oz/28 g	4 Tb	
Dairy			
Butter	8 oz/250 g	1 C	2 sticks
Cheese, cheddar, Swiss	4 oz/125 g	1 C grated	
Cheese, Parmesan,	4 oz/125 g	¾ C grated	
Crème fraîche	14 oz/400 g	1 ½ C heavy cream + ¼ C sour cream	
Fruits & Nuts			
Apples	1 lb/500g		3 medium
Banana	1 lb/500 g		3 medium
Pears	1 lb/500 g		3 medium
Grapefruit	14 oz/400g		1 medium
Lemons	1 lb/500 g	1 C juice	4
Limes	1 lb/500 g	½ C juice	6 medium
Oranges	1 lb/500 g	1 C juice	2 medium
Raisins, currants	5 oz/150 g	1 C	
Prunes	7 oz/200 g	1 C	20

	Weight oz/g	Volume	Other Equivalents
Nuts			
Almonds	5 oz/150 g	1 C chopped	
Almonds, ground	4 oz/125 g	1 C	
Coconut (shredded)	4 oz/125 g	1 ¼ C	
Pecans and walnuts	5 oz/150 g	1 C chopped	
Pine nuts	5 oz/150 g	1 ¼ C	
Meat			
Bacon, slab	1 lb/500 g	2 C diced	20 slices
Chicken, bone-in	1 lb/500 g	1 C cooked, diced	
Chicken, breast, boneless	1 lb/500 g	3 C, cooked, diced	4 halves
Chicken thigh, boneless	1 lb/500 g		5–7 pieces
Ground beef/lamb	1 lb/500 g	2 C	
Italian sausage	1 lb/500 g		4 medium
Vegetables			
Avocado	1 lb/500 g	2 ½ C diced	2 medium
Beans (dried)	1 lb/500 g	3 C	
Beets (cooked)	1 lb/500 g		3 medium
Cabbage	3 ½ lb/1 ½ kg	4 qt shredded	1 head
Cucumber, English	1 lb/500 g		1 medium
Carrot	1 lb/500 g	3-4 C shredded	5 medium
Celery	1 lb/500 g	4 C diced	2–4 stalks
Eggplant	1 lb/500 g		1 large
Endive	1 lb/500 g	6 C chopped	4 medium
Fennel	12 oz/400 g		1 medium bulb
Garlic		½ C chopped	25 cloves/2 heads
Garlic		1 head	10–15 cloves
Leeks	1 lb/500 g	6 C sliced	4 large
Lettuce/Mixed greens			
Per serving	2 oz (50 g)		
For 25 servings	3 lb (1 ½ kg)		
For 100 servings	13 lb (6 kg)		
Mushrooms	1 lb/500 g	5 C sliced	20 medium
Onions	1 lb/500 g	2 C chopped	4 medium
Green onions	1 lb/500 g	1 ½ C chopped	16 medium

	Weight oz/g	Volume	Other Equivalents
Peppers, (red, green)	1 lb/500 g	1 ½ C chopped	2 medium
Potatoes	1 lb/500 g		2–3 medium
Rice	1 lb/500 g	2 C	
Shallots	8 oz/250 g	1 ¼ C chopped	10 medium
Spinach (fresh)	1 lb/500 g	1 ½ C cooked	
Spinach (frozen)	10 oz/300 g	1 ½ C cooked	
Tomatoes (fresh)	1 lb/500 g	2 C diced	3 medium
Tomatoes (canned)	29 oz/765 g	3 ⅓ C	1 large can
Zucchini	1 lb/500 g		3 medium

Herbs
Dried

	Weight oz/g	Volume	Other Equivalents
Basil, herbes de Provence, oregano, thyme	2 oz/60 g	½ C	

Fresh

	Weight oz/g	Volume	Other Equivalents
Parsley	4 oz/125 g	1 C chopped	1 bunch
Cilantro	2 ½ oz/75 g	1 C chopped	1 bunch
Mint	3 oz/100 g	1 C chopped	1 bunch
Chives	2 ½ oz/75 g	½ C chopped	1 bunch
Thyme	4 oz/125 g	1 C leaves	1 bunch

Miscellaneous

	Weight oz/g	Volume	Other Equivalents
Bread crumbs	3 ½ oz/100 g	1 C	4 sandwich slices
Bread croutons	3 oz/90 g	1 C	
Cookie crumbs	3 ½ oz/100 g	1 C	12(3") cookies
Mustard, Dijon	8 oz/250 g	1 C	

OVEN TEMPERATURES

US/Metric

Heat level	Fahrenheit	Centigrade
Warm	300	150
Moderate	325	165
Moderately hot	350	175
Hot	425	220

MEASURES

Cups and Spoons	Liquid ounces	Liquid grams
1 teaspoon		5 grams
3 teaspoons = 1 tablespoon		15 grams
2 tablespoons	1 ounce	30 grams
16 tablespoons = 1 cup	8 ounces	227 grams
2 cups =1 pint	16 ounces = 1 pound	454 grams
4 cups = 2 pints = 1 quart	32 ounces	907 grams
4 1/3 cups		1 kilogram (1000 grams)

For convenience using large quantity recipes, the following equivalents are approximate.
8 tablespoons = 125 grams
1 cup = 250 grams
1 pound = 500 grams
1 quart = 1 liter
1 bottle wine or liquor = 750 milliters

ABBREVIATIONS

C	cup(s)	g	gram(s)
lb	pound(s)	kg	kilogram(s)
oz	ounce(s)	ml	milliliter(s)
qt	quart(s)	L	liter(s)
tsp	teaspoon(s)		
Tb	tablespoon(s)		

INDEX OF RECIPES

About the Authors

Thanks to the happy magic of Jim Haynes, the trio of authors, Mary Bartlett, Antonia Hoogewerf, and Catherine Monnet met in Paris, far from their countries of origin. Finding inspiration in between sautéeing onions and stewing Moroccan chicken, the Sunday night dinners were an idea that clearly deserved to be shared.

Mary Bartlett divides her time between Portland, Oregon and Paris. A culinary world traveler, she has the ability to make everyone feel at home. In Oregon, her large, extended family keeps her busy cooking everything from Oysters Rockefeller to organic baby food. In Paris, Mary is a regular cook at the Sunday night dinners. A long time supporter of local and sustainable cooking practices, Mary also writes a cooking blog challenging readers to partake of the joys of simple, healthful and, most importantly, delicious, home cooking while offering practical suggestions and *unintimidating* recipes suitable for all. Her professional experience as a restaurant cook, caterer, and cooking teacher has been vital in creating this practical entertainment guide.

Antonia Hoogewerf stepped in when one of Jim's longtime cooks departed and became a regular chef for his dinners. First and foremost, "mère de famille" and home entertainer, Antonia also owned a 'Chambres d'Hôte' in the Loire Valley for several years, where managing large meals for crowds became second nature. Now living between Paris and Calcutta, with a dash of London thrown in, she travels, writes, orchestrates European walking tours, and cooks for fun. Antonia's primary culinary passion is for India and the many Indian dishes in this book are from her delightful repertoire.

Catherine Monnet arrived in Paris from Los Angeles as a young dancer in 1978, eager to explore her passions for ballet and philosophy. Through a friend, she found temporary lodging at Jim's and, in return for his generosity, she offered to cook for him and his many friends. Voilà, the beginning of the now-legendary, Sunday night dinners! She is currently living and working in Shanghai with her husband, Yves, but Paris will always be home. While raising two sons, completing a doctorate in philosophy at the Sorbonne and still working hard in the ballet studio, Catherine has found time to cultivate that culinary interest that spurred her to help start these weekly soirées at Jim's. She loves to throw large parties, experiment with new cuisine, and write about food and cooking.

978-0-595-43789-4
0-595-43789-3